LIVING BETWEEN CULTURES

FROM BORINQUEN TO HOLLYWOOD

L. A. RIVERA COLÓN

Living Between Cultures:
From Borinquen to Hollywood

Published by Borinquen Media, LLC

Events, locales, and conversations included in this book are from the author's memories, imagination, and conversations with family and friends. To maintain anonymity, in some instances, the author has changed the names of individuals, places, identifying characteristics, and details of his AmeRICAN journey.

Cover design by Rosean Lindsey

Library of Congress Control Number: 2020917930

ISBN —978-1-7356333-0-5

Dedication

There are three very special people I consider my earthly guardian angels who helped shape my life in a deeply profound way:

My mother, Rosa

who demonstrated much love and strength providing me the opportunity and guidance to seek the AmeRICAN Dream.

My beautiful wife, Norma

Thank you for your profound dedication to our family through your limitless and selfless love and grace.

And, my dear friend, Maria Pruetzel

who taught me how to have faith and understand my true purpose in life.

Guardian angels have been defined as spiritual hosts entrusted to care and guide an individual, group, and even countries. I thank God for sending some of His earthly angels to show me kindness and help guide me through my journey.

It is with great honor that I dedicate this memoir to my guardian angels.

CONTENTS

i

PART THREE—THE OTHER SIDE

INTRODUCTION

For over a century, citizens gifted to us by the "Island of Enchantment" have been intricately woven into the American tapestry. Even though innumerable accolades have been received for our achievements in every conceivable vocation, most fellow Americans are sadly unaware of the accomplishments and essential contributions of the Borinquen segment of the Hispanic community.

This memoir began as an attempt to provide my children and their children with a partial history of the hopes, challenges, and successes of our family. In revisiting the chapters of our sojourn, I was forced to wrestle with a myriad of emotions that had lain dormant for many years. As a cleansing balm, this regression into our past served as part of a personal healing process. Through the research undertaken, a better understanding of the motives and challenges faced by my family members emerged. Reliving their struggle for daily survival helped me revisit the beauty of our Puerto Rican heritage, culture, and faith.

It could be said that most of us travel along life's road trying to better ourselves and provide for our loved ones. We strive to become the best we can be. However, we will all face our own crossroads forcing us to make life-altering decisions, which can bring economic, moral, and spiritual success ... or disaster. My decision-making process was dramatically changed at a very critical time in my life. I am pleased to share my journey with you.

PART ONE

Sand and Sea

LIVING BETWEEN CULTURES

Chapter 1

ISLAND OF ENCHANTMENT

It was early April 1949, and the waves broke on the sandy beach near Santa Isabel, Puerto Rico, with the soothing sound of centuries past. Along the southern horizon, the faint colors of dawn lightened the sky as a solitary figure made her way along the shore. A closer look revealed a young woman of startling beauty, barely nineteen years of age, a burlap sack in one hand and a machete in the other.

Rosa Colón Aponte had the looks of a young movie star, but she was no actress and her life was no movie. She was struggling, literally, to survive. She walked barefoot across the sandy beach, her glance sharp, her ears attentive, checking homemade tin traps for blue-tipped land crabs or *cangrejos* that had crawled inside the rusting square cracker cans and now sought escape.

After an hour or so of emptying her catch into a brown burlap sack, she paused to look at the sea. It spread before her like a sheltering mother. Allowing herself a slight smile, she turned from the rolling surf and made her way to the small house on stilts where she lived with her husband, Tomás Rivera. She had married Tomás, a widower and twenty-four years her senior, over the objections of her mother, *Doña* (Mrs.) Eugeñia. While Eugeñia had much respect for Tomás, she could see no future in the marriage. The difference in their ages was great, and she wondered how her daughter would cope with the responsibilities of raising five children, the oldest of whom wasn't far from her own age.

Most other couples in love followed the tradition of that time when singles would meet while strolling chaperoned under the shade of the manicured, umbrella-shaped trees lining the town's plaza. Rosa and Tomás were brought together out of economic necessity. Rosa had known little but hard work as the oldest daughter in a family of two boys and seven girls. She had foregone most of her schooling to help the family survive the harsh economic effects of the aftermath of the Great Depression during the 1930s and 1940s. Caring for five stepchildren was not much different from shouldering the responsibilities she had borne with her younger siblings. Furthermore, her marriage to Tomás had taken on a new dimension. Rosa was pregnant with me, her first child.

The wealthy folks of Santa Isabel lived near the center of town in homes with ornate wrought-iron porches near the plaza facing the Catholic Church, Santiago Apóstol, which provided its blessings to the faithful from birth to death. In comparison, coconut-laden palm trees surrounded my family's little piece of the island near the beach community, known as El Cocal (the Coconut Grove). My family's lack of money was offset by the plentiful *cocos* (coconuts) that we used as a source of food, water, dishware, and fuel. The green outer husk that covers the inner coconut, when dried, was converted to charcoal for cooking.

As Mom reached her small wooden house, she emptied her catch into a chicken-wire corral where the crabs would feed on morsels of coconut for several days to clean out their digestive system and sweeten their taste. With a little luck, she'd succeed in convincing tourists to sit down for a royal feast of crabs served with white rice and red beans or a garnish of *tostones* (fried plantains), washed down with fresh coconut water. At times it got too hot near the coals and I would kick, wanting to be born sooner than expected. Mom would gently pass her hand over her belly while talking to me and continue cooking.

However, a dollar from the odd tourist passing by could not be expected to cover the entire family's needs. While Dad worked from approximately January to May, from sunset to nearly sundown as a *picador de caña* (sugarcane cutter), his pay alone was likewise inadequate to feed so many mouths. Thank God for the fruit trees and coconut palms in the yard, as well as the occasional help from *Tía* Santa (Dad's youngest sister), who owned a small grocery store in the *colonia* (colony) where she lived. Even in nearby Ponce, Puerto Rico's second largest city, everyone seemed to be reeling from the harsh economic times, except for the rum distillery owners who had a growing local and international market.

While there was a daily struggle to survive, there were few complaints considering the beauty of the island and bounty of its fertile land. Poverty could not take away the sunny days scented by the aroma of coffee and the majestic sight of the fields of tall, green sugar cane swaying softly as if dancing a *bolero* with the tropical breezes.

On a typical day, Mom would prepare Dad his breakfast then get the younger children ready for school. She would personally escort them to the schoolhouse; she in front and the children in single file behind her. Some of the neighbors liked to joke that Mom looked like a mother hen leading her chicks—even though a few of them rose above her in height!

Later in the morning, Mom cooked flan (custard) or *pasteles de carne* (meat pies) to sell in the *colonia*. She also took in laundry from the financially better-off folks like Vidal Morales Cintron, the mayordomo (manager) of the sugar company who employed many of the area residents. Once all her household duties were done, if she had any extra time, Mom would prepare for her baby's arrival.

She had already sewn together a good supply of diapers from assorted clean rags when she went into labor in the fall of 1949. It had been a long, hot summer and the sweltering heat was still in full force. Early signs indicated it would be a difficult delivery. Mom could have gone to the small hospital in the center of Santa Isabel, but she was prudish by nature and recoiled at the thought of a male orderly seeing her naked. Since Dad could not afford a private doctor, that left one option—the village midwife.

A few hours past midnight, with the village midwife in attendance, a male child came screaming and kicking into the "paradise" of El Cocal. I was named after Mom's older brother, Luis, as a sign of respect which, later in life, would strike me as odd given that the two of them quarreled so much in their youth.

Dad fished about in his pockets to pay the midwife her fee, and then looked under his thin mattress for the three dollars she was owed. He already knew he didn't have the money. Preparations for the sugarcane cutting season would not begin until December, and three dollars was the greater portion of a week's pay for a cane cutter. Nonetheless, he went through the motions in believable fashion. Coming up short, he smiled and asked the midwife if a goat would be acceptable instead.

The midwife's eyes narrowed. Dad was not a handsome man physically, but, like the French literary character Cyrano de Bergerac, he was witty and exuded a casual charm that stood him in good graces with most people, especially the ladies. However, the midwife was not given much to manners or flattery. She was already suspicious but nodded reluctantly.

Dad excused himself and returned with a crippled goat worth a dollar (if that). The midwife turned purple with rage and launched into a barrage of curses, drowning out my cries and casting a shadow over the domestic scene. She finally stormed from the house in a huff, dragging the poor goat behind her.

Naturally, I was oblivious to it all, safe and secure in my mother's arms. Dad sighed deeply, sitting on an old wooden crate and looking with concern at me—his sixth child. Gradually, all became quiet save the gentle breathing of my mother and me, and the soothing, rhythmic chirping of the tiny *coquí* frogs all around. Dad stepped outside to look at the star-filled sky. He had nothing to compare it to, but something deep inside told him he was privileged to behold such beauty. He allowed the steady, gentle sea breeze and the rustling of the palm fronds to soothe his frayed nerves.

Off in the distance, he discerned the outline of the old hacienda owned by the Alomar family from Spain. They had come to Puerto Rico from the island of Majorca early in the nineteenth century. Nearly a dozen families now lived in one room *cuarteles* (barracks) built nearby and in the original brick *almacén* (warehouse), which had fallen into disrepair and was now used to store fertilizer for the cane fields. The area in general was known as Colonia Alomar.

A *ruiseñor* (nightingale) sang in the darkness, and Dad imagined the toasts that would be made later in the day with cups of *pitorro* (homemade rum) passed among family and friends. There would be shouts of joy at the birth of a son and jokes made of Dad being old enough to be my grandfather.

Dad shuddered involuntarily. The curses of the outraged midwife hung over his head like the sulfurous smell of the fertilizer stored in the *almacén* at Alomar–a pungent odor blamed for the respiratory ailments afflicting many in the *colonia*, including my grandmother, Eugeñia, or Geña, as she was called.

Dad looked at his frail house and shook his head. He had to do better. He had to do better for his family. He had to do better for his newborn son feeding at his wife's breast. He was a man, after all, and though he was getting on in age, there was still time to act. There was still time to make a difference.

The *ruiseñor* chirped more emphatically in the darkness.

"That bird seems busy about something," he murmured.

After lingering awhile, Dad finally turned and walked inside the cramped, one-bedroom house. A few minutes later, he was lulled into a deep sleep by the tiny *coquí's* serenade.

Chapter 2

THE AMERICAN DREAM

With its fern-like leaves and flowers in vivid hues of orange-red petals, the *flamboyán* tree, also known as the Royal Poinciana, is common throughout Puerto Rico. When the delicate, paper-like flowers complete their brief lifecycle and fall from the tree, butterflies appear from nowhere, as though accompanying the petals on their final journey to the ground.

The *flamboyán* is also used as a sort of bookmark to celebrate the end of the sugarcane harvest. Workers and their families gathered in the countryside and yoked their oxen to the *carretas*, the sturdy wooden carts used for hauling cut cane from the fields. They tied the flowering branches of the *flamboyán* over the horns of the oxen as well as around the sides of the rumbling carts. Then everyone paraded into town, celebrating *la caravana del acabe* (the caravan of the end of the harvest).

But all that was months earlier, and deplorable poverty had again tightened its grip on the field workers of Santa Isabel. For *picadores de caña* like my father, work in the sugarcane fields was only seasonal, lasting about six months of the year. A fortunate few would remain employed by maintaining farm equipment and preparing for the next cane season, but the second half of the year would be a battle for survival for most. In my father's case, he would give Mom a hand with her brood of chickens or play the national *lotería* by purchasing a *billete* from an elderly peddler selling these paper pieces of hope near Tía Santa's store. Other times, he might go saltwater fishing with his friends or bet on the cockfights in the nearby town of Coamo. In the end, however, Dad did well to break even.

Thankfully, Mom's business acumen never seemed to fail the family. In addition to the extra washing she did for the wealthier families in town, she had a knack for generating income from small things like the *cangrejos* she caught along the seashore or the popular dishes she made from scratch and sold at a profit in the neighborhood.

Then, too, there was the natural fruitfulness of the land that kept many families from outright starvation—the citrus and avocado trees that proliferated in everyone's backyard and the abundant supply of coconuts and mangoes, fresh seafood, and practical help from one's extended family.

It was no surprise to anyone to see Dad and his younger brother, Eduardo, gathered one morning in March 1950 with thirty or so men from nearby towns. They had turned out to meet the American recruiter who had come to Ponce to hire contract laborers for farm work in the USA. There always seemed to be a shortage of laborers for this backbreaking work in the states. In fact, Puerto Ricans were being recruited to work in farms as far away as Hawaii.

The heavyset *Americano* sat in the government office studying the thin, ill-clad men in front of him. Though he had dressed all in white to ward off the effects of the tropical sun, he still sweated profusely. Beside him was a translator, a slim, wiry man with a thin neatly trimmed black mustache and military posture.

"This is a time of hardship for many," began the *Americano*, speaking through the interpreter. "The world is in flux ..." The interpreter hesitated and looked at the *Americano*, clearly confused with the meaning of "flux."

"Change," said the *Americano*. "The world is changing, and times are hard."

When haven't they been hard? thought Dad, half-absentmindedly.

"I can tell just by lookin' at your hands that you men are hard-workin' fellas," continued the *Americano*. "You're used to workin' the land. After all, your southern coastal towns are known for agriculture. And that's good 'cause the jobs we're offering in the U. S. of A. require men who understand the soil ... men who know what it means to sweat over their labor and not sit behind some desk in an air-conditioned office pushin' paper back and forth."

The *Americano* wiped the sweat from his brow with a handkerchief as the translator struggled to find the right words.

"Now, I know that most'a you boys are busy cuttin' sugarcane half the year," continued the recruiter, "but with nuthin' to do the rest'a the year. Well, I'm here to change that picture for you if you're willin' to do your part."

The *Americano* shifted in his seat and Dad felt he was speaking directly to him when he said, "You can come to the U. S. of A. and work all year long if you like, makin' better pay over there than you'll ever get cuttin' cane here in Puerta Rico ..."

The *Americano* continued to talk steadily for the next several minutes extolling the virtues of life and work on the mainland, and, as Dad and the other men in line already knew, not without justification. Over the years, tens of thousands of Puerto Ricans had migrated to the United States for work. Many of them had prospered in their second country.

The *Americano* paused and looked around him. "Our world is a dangerous place," he said, "and many nations are strugglin' to make ends

16

meet. But America will stick by her friends. My country has always been the friend of the Puerto Rican people ..."

This last claim was debatable by some. Dad had only attended a few years of grade school, but he knew full well that thousands of Boricuas, led primarily by the independence movement's Dr. Pedro Albizu Campos and his Nationalist party, would disagree with the *Americano's* bold assertions. However, Tomás, wasn't standing in line to join a debate on the political status of his homeland with the U.S. nor were the men around him. Theirs was a constant struggle to find bread to feed their families.

The details were straightforward enough. If accepted for employment, Tomás and the others would sign a contract, fly to the United States, and work in the northeastern part of the country in places with strange names like Con-nec-ti-cut, De-la-ware, Penn-syl-va-nia, and Mas-sa-chu-setts. The cost of air travel, as well as room and board in the States, would automatically be deducted from their earnings to reimburse the company. After that, each man was free to save as much money as he could and send it home to his loved ones.

The *Americano* grew teary as he described the natural beauty of his native land. The endless fields of tobacco and cotton, the sweet-smelling apple orchards, and row upon row of brightly colored vegetables requiring picking ...

"From sea to shining sea," proclaimed the *Americano*. He stood and knocked over a rickety chair next to him. He pulled back and forth on his suspenders, as the translator stooped to pick up the chair and a stack of papers that had scattered on the ground. "The U. S. of A. is a workers' paradise!" added the *Americano*, rocking on his heels. And then, either impatient with the translator, or eager to show off some Spanish of his own, he exclaimed in a loud voice, "*¡Un paradiso! ¡Un paradiso!*" using the Italian word for paradise instead of the Spanish *paraíso*.

The recruiter sat back down and wiped his forehead with his handkerchief while signaling with his other hand for the men to approach the table in a single line for questioning. When it came time for Dad to sign his contract, he did not hesitate, scratching out his name laboriously in several places on the documents. Then he shook the recruiter's hand and turned to walk away. His whole life was about to change! He went to his parents' house first to tell them the news, later heading home to Mom and the kids. That night, once the children had gone to sleep, he asked Mom to walk outside with him, so they could talk further.

"How long will you be gone?" Mom asked.

Dad stared at her. All he could think about was how beautiful she looked in the moonlight.

"How long will you be gone?" she repeated impatiently.

Dad cleared his throat. "Dance with me," he said.

Mom gently pushed him away. She was tired and wanted to sleep. She would be too busy to count the days of his absence anyway. "And make sure you send some money home," she added. "Otherwise, I'll go to the mainland myself to find you!"

Many husbands from that era would have had stern words for their wife's impertinence, but Dad smiled all the more. His wife seemed like a hard nut to crack because of the tough life she lived, but he was not one to give up easily. Patience and gentleness marked his overall approach to life. After telling Mom how beautiful she looked and how helpless he was to refuse her every command, he pulled her close and kissed her passionately. Mom struggled for a moment and then submitted.

As if reading her thoughts, Dad pulled back and smiled. "I love you, Rosín," he said. "You make me happy!" And with that, he began to sing,

"Your beauty is like a rose. Rosíta, my precious flower ..."

"Oh, lower your voice!" Mom said, walking toward the house.

But Dad sang all the louder, dancing an impromptu bolero on the white sand.

Mom turned at the top of the steps. "You'll wake up the children!" she insisted.

But her protests were useless. Dad felt the music in his soul, and his feet had a life of their own that he could no more restrain than the sea breeze rustling the fronds of the palm trees. Mom shook her head and allowed herself a smile. It was crazy. The whole thing was crazy, and life was much too hard. What was there to dance about anyway? But she could not deny her love for this man, even if he was old enough to be her father. She walked down the steps and joined Dad in his bolero on the glistening white sand which spread under their feet without blemish in the silver light of the moon.

Chapter 3

THE MAINLAND

A month or so later, Dad climbed aboard a Douglas DC-3 twin engine airplane parked on a runway at the edge of town along with his brother, Eduardo, and a dozen or so other men from Santa Isabel and neighboring towns. Because of Puerto Rico's commonwealth relationship with the United States, making them U.S. citizens, they wouldn't need passports or special documents to travel to and from the mainland, and so the loading process went quickly.

Once on board, Dad entertained his fellow passengers with jokes and stories, but grew quiet as the airplane's engines powered up. The great bird shook and rattled down the runway with a deafening roar. He stole glances at his fellow passengers and tried to keep himself from showing his anxiety. Many of them had never been on an airplane. Filiberto Godoy had flown before and shouted melodramatically at his companions to remain calm.

As the plane abruptly achieved liftoff, Dad looked down at the armrest and realized that Eduardo had joined him in tightening their grip. He peeked through the window at the receding cane fields and town of Santa Isabel, and allowed himself to breathe a little. Even the mountains were beginning to appear small and insignificant, as the DC-3 continued its raucous ascent, passing through billowy white clouds that shook the plane every so often and prompted Tomás to seek some heavenly confidence by praying silently. He wasn't the type of believer who spoke of God often, but he made his humble request for protection of his loved ones until they reunited, and for his success as he made his way to this mysterious new land that held so much hope for the future.

Finally, the airplane leveled off, and the captain set his course northward. The men on board began to relax and someone called out to Dad, "Hey, Tomás, finish that story!"

Dad spoke deliberately in a low voice so he could barely be heard, and the idea of him telling a story was abandoned. Everyone settled back, and the plane was soon over the blue waters of the Caribbean Sea.

After changing aircraft in Miami, Dad's plane headed farther north, touching down in Baltimore, Maryland, where the men were met by a drab, olive-green school bus for the ride north to the farmlands of Pennsylvania. The weather was cool and rainy, and Dad gazed out the window at the passing scenery.

So many cars. So many people. And the roads so wide and smooth ...

Dad's stomach rumbled, and he wondered when he would get something to eat. He had been told his new employers would provide him three meals a day. Something pressed against his shoulder, and he turned to see Eduardo sound asleep and using Dad as a cushion. Dad shifted and so did Eduardo, making himself more comfortable against his older brother's arm and shoulder.

Dad smiled. He had always been a protector for his younger brother and that did not change in the days and months ahead. Dusk began to settle by the time the school bus reached the dirt road leading to the barracks where they would be housed. Conversations among the men grew more animated as they neared a clearing where several large, wood-framed buildings stood behind a chain-link fence.

"What is this?" asked Eduardo. "We are so far from the town."

Two Latinos waited for the new arrivals. One was Edgar Laval, a tall man from Chihuahua, Mexico. Edgar claimed that, when he was a little boy, he had seen Pancho Villa driving by the Laval house with his bodyguard the day Villa was gunned down in an ambush in the town of Parral.

The other man was Ramiro Chávez, short of stature and soft-spoken. He was from Chiapas in southern Mexico. He spoke fairly good English, and the farm bosses depended on him to communicate with the new workers who could only speak Spanish.

Ignacio Miranda, one of the men from Santa Isabel who had traveled with Tomás, could scarcely contain his excitement at meeting Mexican people since Mexican movies were all the rage throughout the Caribbean and Latin America in general. "I've seen every movie Cantinflas has ever been in!" he boasted.

Another of the Puerto Ricans, Juanito Franco, chimed in, "I've been in love with Dolores Del Río since I was a youngster! Do you know her?" Del Río was the first major Latina star to succeed in Mexico and Hollywood.

The men around Juanito scoffed, and one man tapped Juanito playfully on the head.

Filiberto Godoy shouted, "How do you expect them to know Dolores Del Río personally?"

"I don't know her," remarked Edgar coolly, "but I once met Katy Jurado at a party in Guadalajara." That got everyone's attention as the sultry Jurado was one of the most popular Mexican film, stage, and movie actresses of the day. Edgar added, "My uncle's brother-in-law's cousin is the aunt of the personal secretary to the governor of Jalisco."

The men from Santa Isabel stared at Edgar blankly.

"Jalisco is the state in México where Katy was born. Don't you guys know that?" Edgar asked.

The Puerto Ricans shook their heads, and broad smiles crept across their faces. The lengthy genealogy and unfamiliarity of Mexican geography confused them, but they realized one thing: This man knew Katy Jurado! As could be expected, a celebrity status began to grow quickly around the tall Mexican from Chihuahua.

After dinner, Dad and the other men broke off into pairs, choosing the narrow bunk beds where they would be sleeping. The beds were placed military fashion around the barracks with a cast iron wood-burning stove located in the middle of the room. Dad and Tío Eduardo chose to bunk together with Tío Eduardo sleeping on the top bed because, as Tomás put it, his legs were "younger."

Work began bright and early the following morning in the sprawling apple orchards. It was demanding work, but it didn't take long for the new arrivals from Borinquen to get the hang of it. Borinquen is the Spanish version of the native Taíno's name for Puerto Rico—*Borikén* (the land of the valiant and noble lord). Some of the laborers had previously worked on fruit, nursery, and tobacco farms in other states. Dad was assigned to help in the warehouse.

When the heat of summer became more intense and the working hours expanded to twelve and fourteen hours a day, Dad realized how fortunate he was to be indoors tending to the tools and equipment needed by the workers. Summer waned, and the nights grew cooler. Several months passed, and Dad managed to pay off his airfare and was able to send a few dollars home each week to Mom. But despite his "success," he began to feel restless. Something told him there were new horizons to discover. Besides, he was getting too old for this backbreaking work.

That night, as the men were turning in after a hard day's work, Juanito called out to Dad to tell them a story. Over the past few months, Dad had developed the habit of coming up with stories once or twice a week—at first just for Tío Eduardo and the men sleeping nearest them—but now everyone in the barracks wanted to hear his stories. No one would admit it, but hearing my dad tell stories inevitably created a soothing effect while evoking fond memories of their homeland.

Dad cleared his throat and raised his voice loud enough for everyone to hear. "There was a man from Cayey," he began, referring to a town in central Puerto Rico that all his listeners would recognize. "And this man had a really smart, beautiful green parrot he taught to say, '¡Sin dudas!'" ("No doubt about it!")

Dad waited a few moments as several of the men whistled and laughed in anticipation of the story. Others shouted for quiet and Dad continued. "Well, this man got an idea, see, to go around the village when no one was looking and bury some gold coins here and there. Then the next day, he walked around with the parrot on his shoulder, showing him off to everyone and saying, 'Hey! Look how smart my bird is. He can even tell me where to look for hidden money!' And with that, people from the village gathered around to see what would happen. 'Oh, wise parrot,' said the man. 'Tell me ... shall I dig here for money?'

"Br-r-a-a-w-k!!" cried Dad in the dark, imitating the parrot's squawk. "¡Sin dudas!" There were chuckles from the men in the barracks; everyone was listening now.

"Well," Dad, continued, "as you might expect, the man dug into the ground near his feet and right away found some gold coins much to the excitement of the villagers. 'What an amazing bird!' they said to each other.

"Now, one of the people watching happened to be a lazy young man who thought he was too smart to have to work for a living. And he followed the owner of the parrot around, watching him continue to ask the parrot where to look for gold coins here and there buried in the ground. So, the young man decided he had to have this parrot as his own. He was desperate to get it! 'How much do you want for that bird?' he asked impatiently. And the owner said, 'A hundred dollars.'

"'No, no, no!' argued the lazy young man. 'That's too much money!'

"But the owner held firm on his price. He wouldn't sell his parrot for a penny less, and so the young man, wanting to be rich without working, agreed to pay the price. He sold everything he had to buy that old bird, and then went around town asking the parrot to guide him to all the places where money was hidden in the ground. But, of course, he never found anything and finally came to the realization he had been tricked. *¡Sin dudas!*' squawked the parrot loudly.

"And you know what happened then?" asked Tomás.

Juanito called out, "What happened?"

Dad waited a little for dramatic effect. "Well, the young man was lazy, it's true, but he also had a sense of humor. He looked at the parrot and laughed. 'I guess I need to get to work, don't I?' said the young man. 'After all, that's the best way to earn money, right?' To which the parrot replied in a raspy voice, *'¡Sin dudas!'*"

Dad heard a few of the men chuckling appreciatively in the darkness. Then there was quiet, apart from some of the men snoring softly.

Tío Eduardo spoke from the bunk bed above Dad. *"Gracias por el cuento, hermano. Buenas noches."* ("Thanks for the story, brother. Goodnight.")

"Buenas noches," said Dad. He lay awake awhile longer, thinking of Mom and the family back in Santa Isabel. He imagined their voices and laughter and prayed everyone had enough to eat. He squinted out the window, but there was nothing to see. Outside, all was dark, and no stars shone in the sky. From the side of a barn, faint light came from a solitary bulb that would burn throughout the night. Pulling his blanket tighter around him, Dad turned on his side and sighed deeply. "Tomorrow, I will need to go to work, *sin dudas."*

And hearing the hoot of an owl somewhere in the distance, he fell asleep.

LIVING BETWEEN CULTURES

Chapter 4

MIGRATING WITHIN AMERICA

Mom found a money order and a letter from Dad waiting for her at the post office in mid-December. She studied the postal money order from Dad right away and made sense of the numbers. She nodded with satisfaction at the amount he had sent and made the half-hour walk back home, nervously fingering the letter and looking at it often. The stamp had caught her attention immediately, and she was intrigued by the grade-school lettering on the envelope. She did not know how to read, but experience had taught her what her first name looked like: Rosa.

Vitín, the oldest of the five stepchildren, read the letter aloud as Rosa worked in the house.

"Dear Rosín ... I am in East Chicago, Indiana. I am working at a steel factory near a large lake. I am making better money now. I want you to come here. It is very cold. I will send you money for a plane ticket. Love, Tomás."

Mom had Vitín read the letter to her again. And, then a third time, but more slowly. "Where is this place?" she asked Vitín finally. "East of Chicago. Is that where the gangsters live?"

"Gangsters?" asked Vitín.

"You know, Alfonso Capone?"

Vitín shook his head. He said he did not know about gangsters east of Chicago, but he had heard that it did get cold there.

Mom was suddenly upset. Why would Vitín's father pick such a cold place to live and work? And why did he move there first and tell her later? How did he expect her to leave all the children behind to follow him to the edge of a freezing lake where gangsters prowled about?

Vitín's eyes followed Mom, as she paced back and forth, talking to herself. He slipped quietly from the living room while Mom continued to analyze the situation from various angles in quick-fire speech.

"And what am I to do with Cholito?" she mused aloud, referring to me by my nickname. "Am I to leave him here by himself?"

And then, as if on cue—or so they tell me—I waltzed into the room, barely fifteen months of age, and stared up at Mom with big, dark brown eyes.

"*¡Dios mío!*" exclaimed Mom. "He thinks I'm going to leave him behind!" She made the sign of the cross and rushed to pick me up, but not before my half-sister, Guilla, walked past, scooping me up in her arms. From what they say, I laughed and gurgled with delight as Guilla pushed her face into my neck and shoulders and made loud, squealing noises, then carried me down the steps outside to play. Mom was left speechless as I waved goodbye to her.

The suddenness with which it all happened struck Mom as a sign that I would be safe with my half-siblings until I could make my own way to the mainland with more of the family. One day soon, she assured herself, we would all be together again. God would keep the gangsters away, and "Luisito" would grow into a healthy and handsome man. He would get a good education above all and would grow to be respected in the community.

Mom sat near the entrance of the house, watching the children play nearby, their happy shouts drifting toward her like clouds of fragrant incense. She looked around. She was not alone. She had a Mighty Protector—*Dios el Todopoderoso*. Feeling the sure and steady presence of the Divine, she laughed and cried at the same time, her tears like the rain that falls suddenly after a long and oppressive drought.

The month taken to prepare for the trip was not long enough to please Mom. There were too many arrangements to be made. But when the final day came, she departed for the United States wearing a plain cotton dress and carrying a small worn suitcase. Like Dad, she had never been in an airplane, but, unlike him, she felt exhilaration at being airborne, especially at the sight of the emerald green sea sparkling in the sunlight beneath her.

After clearing customs in Miami, she flew north and west, arriving in Chicago early Saturday evening. My jubilant father met her at the airfield, hugged and kissed her, and immediately bundled her up in an oversized jacket he had bought the day before.

"Come on, Rosín," he said. "Let's get you to the car."

They walked outside the passenger terminal. Dad didn't see his ride, so he and Mom started down the sidewalk. They had gone less than fifty feet when a loud whistle pierced the air. Dad saw his friend, Rolando Cruz, standing across the street, waving.

"Over here!" Rolando shouted.

"Who's that?" asked Mom.

"That's our driver," said Dad, wrapping Mom tighter in the billowing coat and ushering her across the dividers to where Rolando stood waiting proudly beside his 1938 Plymouth coupe.

Rolando was a short, stocky man with a black mustache and a large gap between his two front teeth. He smiled broadly as Mom and Dad drew nearer and opened the car door for them to get inside. Dad made a brief introduction and helped Mom into the car. Then they left for East Chicago, just across the border in Indiana, where Dad lived in an all-male boarding house near the Inland Steel Mill.

Dad chatted incessantly along the way, pointing out various landmarks he had come to know over the last several months. An hour later, as Rolando turned down Block Avenue and approached the boarding house, he honked the horn repeatedly.

"What's the matter?" asked Dad. "Why are you honking your horn like that?"

"Everyone's expecting your arrival, Tomás!" exclaimed Rolando.

"My arrival? What do you mean?"

"Perhaps I should say the arrival of the *señora*!" exclaimed Rolando, grinning widely.

"Who did you tell?"

"Everyone!" said Rolando. "This is a big occasion!"

"Stop honking your horn like you're in a parade and pull into the alley over there," Dad ordered his friend.

"The alley?" responded Rolando.

35

"Just do as I say," said Dad.

Rolando parked in the alleyway behind the boarding house. But if Dad thought they had escaped detection from the other boarders, he was mistaken. Alerted by the car horn, several dozen men leaned out of their windows or stood on the fire escape to get a good look at Tomás and his newly arrived wife.

"¡*Oyeme*, Tomás! *¡Te ves bien, amigo, con la señora!*" ("Hey, Tomás! You're looking good with the missus, friend!")

"*Ya era tiempo, ¿Cierto?*" ("It's about time, really!")

Echoing chaotically off the walls of the surrounding buildings, shouts and whistles and greetings were mixed and thrown together like a hastily wrapped birthday gift. Dad lowered his head and hurried Mom to a side door leading to the basement.

"Who are those men?" Mom asked, as they walked slowly in the dark hallway.

"They live here, too, *mi amor*. Most of them work with me at the steel plant," Dad responded airily. "But we're off work today."

"And I have to sleep in the same building with ... them?"

"No, no, no Rosín! I've got us our own special place!"

"Where is that?"

36

"Down here," said Dad, opening another door onto a wooden staircase that descended into a dark abyss.

"I can't see a thing," said Mom, reaching for Dad's hand. "Where're you taking me?"

"Downstairs, *mi amor*. In the basement."

"I have never been to a basement before."

"Oh, this is a rare jewel, *mi amor*. We're so lucky! The furnace keeps it nice and warm down here." Dad found a light switch, flipped it on, and led Mom down the rickety staircase. "Normally, we only have men living in this building, but the landlord has given us permission to sleep down here."

"How much is he charging us?" asked Mom.

"Oh, that's the beauty of it, *mi cielo*. It costs the same as what I paid for my old room! And don't worry about my friends. They're all *caballeros* (gentlemen) at heart."

"Well, it could be worse, but those *caballeros* better mind their manners," she remarked sternly as Dad stepped into yet another dark room and fumbled about for a lightbulb hanging from a cord in the ceiling.

"Close your eyes, *mi cielo*."

"Why? I can't see a thing as it is."

Tomás found the bulb and tightened it in its socket. A yellowish glow dimly lit the room.

"Here you are, Rosín!" exclaimed Dad, pointing around the room, which was basically an open space around a large coal bin.

"What is this?" asked Mom.

"This is where we sleep!" Dad said pointing to a cot nearby.

Rosa walked over to the cot and sat on it. She looked tired. Dad sat gingerly beside her, hoping the cot would not tear from the weight. He put his arm around her, pulling her to him and kissing her neck. Rosa stiffened.

"I'm just happy to see you, Rosín," Dad said, pulling back. "And you're looking so beautiful," he added with a wink.

Mom sighed and allowed Dad to kiss her again. "Do you have any food?" she asked.

"Of course, of course," said Dad, getting to his feet. "I know how long and hard the trip has been. Come on, let's go for a walk."

"I don't want to go out there again, Tomás! I want something to eat!"

"We'll get something to eat, *mi amor*. How would you like real Puerto Rican food? We can go to the restaurant down the street!"

Mom looked with suspicion. "We can buy real Puerto Rican food? Here, east of Chicago?"

"*Mi amor*, there's a whole community of Boricuas living here. We're surrounded by them! Come on, Rosín. You just got here. There's a lot you don't know."

"Like what?"

Tomás smiled and walked around the room. "We're in the states of America, Rosín! This is the land of opportunity and abundance!" Rosa looked impartially at the veneer of coal dust covering everything in the basement. "What about the gangsters?" she asked finally.

"The gangsters?" replied Tomás, unscrewing the solitary light bulb until the room went dark again. "What gangsters?"

"You know, Alfonso Capone."

"You mean, Al Capone. He's been dead a long time, *mi amor.*"

"They shoot him up?"

"No, he got sick and died in Florida."

"Somewhere in Florrrida," mused Mom. "It's a lot warmer down there."

Dad reached for Mom's hand in the darkness. "Life is good here, *mi angel.* You'll see."

Mom continued to voice her misgivings, which were only compounded once they were outside again. A cold wind blew off Lake Michigan and seemed to pierce to her very soul.

Fortunately, it was a short walk to *La Fonda* (the boarding house restaurant), a popular eatery with the steel workers and their families who lived in the neighborhood. Dad had previously told the owners about his wife, and they had agreed to give her a job as a dishwasher once she arrived.

39

Sitting at a table covered with a vinyl checkerboard cloth, Mom had a tasty meal of *pollo asada* (roasted chicken) served with rice and fried plantains and went straight to work. She didn't mind. The kitchen was warm, and the hot water felt good on her hands. More importantly, it allowed her to avoid Dad's friends. Several had followed them from the boarding house with the pretext of wanting to catch a quick bite. They were now all staring at her between endless sips of black *Bustelo* coffee.

"Probably every one of them is married," Mom muttered to herself amid the clattering and banging of pots and pans. "And cheating on their wives."

Dad spent the rest of the afternoon sitting at a table in the restaurant smoking cigarettes with his friends, telling long and entertaining stories, and letting everyone know he was the husband of the beautiful young Boricua working in the kitchen. The one with the looks of a movie star.

Chapter 5

MOM'S HOME COOKING

Despite the unrelenting cold that seemed to bite into Mom like a rabid dog, she was never late for work, gaining the admiration and respect of the restaurant owners as well as her co-workers. One day, during the lunch hour rush, the middle-aged head cook burned a large order of expensive steaks by disappearing through the back door to meet with her boyfriend. She was fired on the spot by the irate owner, and Mom was given her job.

Soon "Chef" Rosa's culinary creations were gracing the restaurant's menu and drawing increasingly more customers as word-of-mouth spread about the pretty Puerto Rican woman's sensational cooking. High on everyone's list was her roast pork and *mofongo* made with mashed plantains and garlic with a special *sofrito* sauce. Other specialties included *arroz con gandules* (rice and pigeon peas), *bacalaítos* (codfish fritters), and steaming bowls of *asopao* soup that sometimes caused grown men to grow teary eyed with delight.

But Mom's creativity in the kitchen was not limited to Puerto Rican recipes alone. She also learned how to prepare delicious Mexican meals, popular among the Mexican steel workers who flocked the restaurant: *fajitas de pollo* (chicken fajitas), *huevos con chorizo* (scrambled eggs and spicy pork sausage), and *menudo* (beef tripe stew) that resembled the Boricua *mondongo* stew. There seemed to be no end to the variety and quality of her cooking.

By May 1951, the winter had grudgingly given way to warmer weather and thoughts turned, naturally enough, to home. On the odd day off, or perhaps late at night, Mom and Dad talked about their plans to return to *Borinquen* one day. My parents weren't complicated people after all. Like untold thousands of migrants who had come before them, as well as the thousands living around them, they cherished the dream of returning one day to their warm island home amid a fanfare of excitement with family and neighbors turning out to greet them. Their pockets would be full of cash and their suitcases bursting with fine new clothes.

They would buy a parcel of land in Santa Isabel and retire on their *Seguro Social* (Social Security) collected from the years of employment on the USA mainland. They would build a small house of concrete cinderblock painted in light pastel colors and sit on the veranda during the evenings, watching their grandchildren and great-grandchildren playing around them. The tropical breezes would wander in from the sea. The *coquí* frogs and nightjar birds would chirp and sing like a hired band playing into the wee hours of the morning, softening the memory of the harsh American winters that had forced their blood to thicken and necks to shorten.

But that was in the future. Maybe even the distant future. The order of the day was to work and work hard. That was the American way. That was the secret of American success and the practical reality behind achieving the American Dream. It was also the only way to afford getting the rest of the family from Puerto Rico to the States.

As summer gave way to autumn and Christmas approached, Mom's nostalgia deepened. She had been away from *Borinquen* for nearly ten months, and Luisito was foremost in her thoughts. How was he doing? Did he talk a lot? Were his grannies and all his aunts, half-sisters, and cousins looking after him properly? Did he cry at night when he went to bed? Did he ask often for his *mamá*? Did he still remember her? Had there been enough time to bond as mother and son?

Dad tried to comfort Mom as best he could, but his touch (so it seemed to her) was at times a little heavy handed, his words too abrupt or shallow to alleviate her unsettled feelings.

"I want Cholito to come here," she said to him flatly one evening.

Dad, who had been shining his shoes in a corner of the basement, turned down the volume on the radio beside him. "What's that?" he asked.

"Luisito ..."

"Yes?"

Mom answered as she stared at the picture. "I want Luisito to come to the States," she repeated.

Dad resumed shining his shoes nonchalantly. "Well, he will come, *mi cielo*. All in good time."

"I want him to come now."

"Don't you think he's still too young for that, *mi amor*?"

Mom shook her head no. Emphatically, no! She wanted Luisito to travel *ayer* (yesterday). It was well past time for him to be with his mother and father. Guilla could bring him, and Pancha, Maso, Guiso and Vitín could follow later.

"But we'll need to find a bigger place," she added.

44

Dad looked around the basement. It seemed big enough to him, especially with a little rearranging, but before he could say anything, Mom continued, "I don't want the baby breathing this coal dust. It's bad for the lungs."

Dad smiled. "Luisito is no longer a baby, *mi amor.*"

Mom nodded and looked at Dad as if noticing him for the first time. She touched her stomach involuntarily and gave him a look that could have only one meaning. Dad stared at her and after a moment tiptoed over to her side, kneeling reverently, taking her hand in his.

For once, she thought, *his grip does not seem so rough.*

Dad began to sing *"Silent Night"* in Spanish.

Noche de paz, noche de amor
Todo duerme en derredor...

Outside, a light snow was falling. Christmas lights strung here and there along the street gave the scene a storybook feel. A boy and girl, walking down the sidewalk with their father, stopped in front of the building as Dad continued to sing. His voice was rich and warm, and, recognizing the melody, the children and their father began to sing along in English.

Shepherds quake at the sight
Glories stream from heaven afar
Heavenly hosts sing Alleluia ...

After a while, the man and his children went on their way, their voices fading in the distance. Dad, too, grew silent, as the snow continued to fall. Filled with a sense of pride, his eyes began to water, and he ran his fingers over Mom's belly.

"My child will be born in the States. He'll be known as the son of Tomás and live a good life—maybe like the wealthy *Americanos* on the mainland. He'll be respected in the community. He'll live the American Dream."

Chapter 6

A NEW HOME AND BROTHER

In April 1952, a Pan American Airlines flight from New York's LaGuardia Airport unloaded its passengers at the ever-busy Chicago Midway terminal. Guilla, with me in her arms, was among the last of the passengers to step off the plane. A year later, Maso, Pancha, and Guiso would join us. I was not yet three years old, but I still remember bits and pieces of the experience, like when lightning strikes in the darkness, briefly illuminating the scene around you. I was dressed in shorts and sandals, and a handstitched shirt my Tía Santa had given me.

As Guilla tells the story, we didn't know where to go or who to look for. We had thought someone was going to meet us when we got off the plane, but no one was there. Once we stepped out onto the sidewalk in front of the terminal, Guilla led us toward the taxi stand to ask for help. I remember hearing about a very tall man tossing his cigarette to the ground and walking toward us. He spoke harshly in a foreign tongue. I couldn't understand a word he said. I only knew I was suddenly afraid and tried to hide between Guilla's legs.

Just then a man with a mustache and a smile came alongside and told us in Spanish to follow him. Guilla hesitated.

"It's all right," he said, still speaking in Spanish. "Your father, Tomás, sent me. I'm his *compadre*, Esteban."

We followed Esteban across the street and clambered into his car. As we began to leave the airport terminal, a policeman on a motorcycle pulled us over. The cab drivers had complained about Esteban, thinking he was taking away some of their business. Esteban had just enough time to warn us all in Spanish not to say a word.

"If the policeman asks you a question, just smile at him," he added hurriedly.

It turned out to be good advice. When Esteban told the policeman we were his children and had just flown in from San Juan, the policeman shined his light on us and asked us questions. All he got out of me was a beaming smile.

An hour or so later, we were reunited with Mom and Dad. They had moved into a first-floor apartment not far from the boarding house. Mama hugged me and cried, taking my hand, and rubbing it over her protruding stomach. The room was filled with people, and it seemed everyone talked all at once.

Suddenly, I was lifted into the air and found myself looking into my father's eyes. He asked if I knew who he was. Before I could answer, he smiled and kissed me, and his tears spilled onto my cheeks and lips. He turned his face to me so I could kiss him, and I gave him a peck. He tasted like the Caribbean Sea.

Music filled the room, and someone put a caramel in my mouth. Everything was strange. Everything was familiar. I was safe at last. I was home.

My brother, Benjamin, was born three months later in July at St. Catherine's Hospital in East Chicago. Dad didn't have to pay a midwife this time thanks to the medical insurance he enjoyed through his job at the Inland Steel Mill. Unlike when I was born, everything was done in a big-city way. Benjy was born in a delivery room, attended by a doctor and nurses dressed in white.

Everyone was thrilled with the new addition to the family, including the neighbors, our distant relatives, and friends of friends. If there's one quality all Puerto Ricans share, it's love and respect for family.

Mom had hoped for a little girl because she felt a female was more likely to care for her when she got older. But once she held Benjy in her arms and began to nurse him, he became the new love of her life. After a few months, she quit her job at *La Frontera* restaurant to care for him fulltime.

Of course, I loved Benjy, too. How could I not? He had a genuinely sweet nature, evident from an early age. I understood I was his older brother. As he grew older and the two of us began to interact more, I got a payoff: I finally had someone closer to my own age to play with!

In general, Benjy was always more *pegado* (attached) to Mom than I was. Mom, perhaps, reinforced that by calling him "Baby" his entire life. On the other hand, I tended to do a lot of things on my own or with Guiso, the half-brother closest to me in age (we were eight years apart).

Some people thought Guiso was a little slow or *un poquito lento*, but I didn't agree. He had a bad sinus condition most of the time, and his ears and nose were often congested. He couldn't hear very well, and he didn't speak much, so I think people came to conclusions about him without examining his condition in depth. He certainly seemed fine to me, and, thankfully, was a very good brother. The two of us quickly adjusted to life in the states. So much was new and different.

50

As you might imagine, one such difference was the freezing weather and icy wind that turned my face numb and caused my eyes and nose to run. We weren't dressed properly for the cold winters. Our parents were more familiar with the way we dressed in the tropics and not familiar with the wool clothing worn in the colder climates.

The physical environment was also different. I saw concrete, glass, and steel everywhere I looked. There were no palm trees in East Chicago. There were no coconuts in the back yard, no juicy mangos, no sand under my bare feet, no songs of tropical birds waking me up in the mornings. Unlike the older folks who reminisced nostalgically about the "good ol' days" and spoke broken English, I was brought to the mainland while very young and learned to adapt quickly. I picked up the English vernacular and the ways of the city effortlessly.

When I started at the Eugene Field Elementary school, there were more Mexican-American kids than any other ethnic group. Some of their families had been in the country for many generations and spoke English just like the *gringos*. They quickly realized I was different. As often happens when a majority group encounters someone "different," I became a target for bullying. It didn't last too long, however. For one thing, I learned to stick up for myself. For another, once they got to know me, they accepted me as one of their own.

Our living quarters in our apartment were cramped. Four of us, Mom, Dad, Benjy, and I slept in one bed. Pancha and Guilla had their own room. Maso and Guiso slept on thin mattresses laid out on the floor that could later be rolled up and put away.

Maso began to fall in with a bad crowd and spent more and more time away from home. When Vitín came in November 1953, he had a room to himself at night—the kitchen.

To help make ends meet, Mom started an in-home restaurant. There were many workers from the steel mill who had been regular patrons at *La Fonda*. When she quit her job there, they hungered for her cooking and voiced it to my father. Up to five at a time would crowd around our small kitchen like ravenous wolves. Most were short of cash and ate on credit for days at a time, paying Mom when they got their pay checks.

They were the first to eat in the evenings when it was time for dinner. I remember standing in the doorway with my stomach growling, watching them chatter happily among themselves as my mother made her final preparations. They grew quiet while she loaded their plates with food. Their knuckles turned white from gripping their knives and forks, poised to cut, break, and tear apart their portions. Once the food was in front of them, they devoured it with obvious pleasure.

Afterward, for those who could afford it, Mom packed brown-bag lunches for the next day. After they were gone, the rest of us got to eat, but it always seemed to me we didn't get the same quantity of food as the workers from the steel mill.

Even with Dad's regular paycheck and Mom's hard work and business acumen, we struggled financially. After a while, we moved farther down Block Avenue to a rundown storefront rented to us as an apartment. Mom complained to the landlord about the exposed electrical wiring in the building, which posed an obvious danger. She wasn't afraid to use her broken English to express herself.

"You fix *esta casa*! Fix it now!"

The landlord ignored her demands. He was in a position of power, and we were at his mercy.

One Saturday, when I was nearly seven years old, Mom sent me and Guiso to old Santiago, *el barbero* (the barber). Santiago was in his late sixties and his barber shop was in the living room of his apartment. There always seemed to be a group of two or three men his age sitting around a table playing a game of double-six dominoes. Between the slapping sounds of the *fichas* (domino stones) hitting the tabletop as the men made their moves, they chatted among themselves.

When Guiso and I walked into the living room, Santiago decided to cut my hair first. I managed to shimmy myself onto a barstool and was wrapped with an old bed sheet that fell to the floor below my feet. He powered up his electric razor and went to work. It wasn't long before I was squirming.

Santiago held the razor close to my ear and growled, *"Tate quieto, muchacho, o te pongo la dita."* ("Be still, boy, or I'll put the gourd bowl on you.")

Santiago had threatened this before. If I wouldn't sit still, he promised to put a bowl made from a hard-skinned, green fruit of a gourd tree over my head and clip around the perimeter resulting in bangs like a girl.

The street-wise barber continued cutting my hair and asking me questions. How was my mom doing, my dad, how were things at school, who was my favorite teacher? When it was Guiso's turn, the line of questioning was different. He asked him about our older brother, Maso, who spent more time on the streets and was getting into bad habits.

"When did you last see him?" Santiago asked Guiso.

"He stops by and eats dinner most days," said Guiso.

Clip-clip went the scissors around Guiso's ears.

"Is it true *la policia* stopped him the other day?"

"I don't know," answered Guiso.

"I saw the police talking to him in the alley over there off Michigan Avenue," said one old man with thick glasses that made his eyes look small and distant. "He must have been shootin' up with those other *sinvergüenzas* (shameless) that hang out around there. He's a *tecato!*"

"Give him some time, Juancho," said another old man, wearing a Chicago Cubs baseball cap and sipping coffee. "He'll see the error of his ways eventually and get clean."

"You think, Paquito?" said the man with the thick eyeglasses. "They don't never leave the *vicio* (bad habit or vice). Let's hope they don't carry him out of here in a box."

An awkward silence followed this last comment. Everyone turned to look at me. The silence continued, and I could feel my face turning red. I had not understood very much of what they had said, but I had understood enough. My half-brother, Maso, was into drugs. He was becoming someone who could not be trusted in the community. It was common knowledge that some drug addicts would steal from their own mothers.

"Guiso, what's a *tecato?*" I asked, as Guiso and I left old Santiago's house.

"A junkie," replied Guiso simply.

"What's a 'junkie?" I asked.

"You know, a heroin addict."

So that was why Dad always questioned Maso about where he was and who he was with. Dad would drink and smoke, like many men in our neighborhood, but he was totally against using illegal drugs, especially heroin.

When I played in the alleyways, I would sometimes see men sticking needles in their arms and injecting a cloudy, watery mixture straight into their veins. It would send chills up my spine. I couldn't stand getting a shot at the doctor's office. Why would anyone want to inject poison into themselves day after day?

It wasn't unheard of for some families in the inner-city to accept as fate or pretend to ignore that one of their family members had become addicted to heroin. Perhaps, they didn't know what else to do or hoped that, somehow, the addict would see the error of his or her ways and kick this life-destroying habit.

On rare occasions some *tecatos* would get religion and would later be found preaching and playing tambourines with the *Pentecostales* on the street corners. If prayers couldn't reach them, eventually a tremendous sadness would overcome the community when we'd hear of a neighbor's son or daughter dying from an overdose. We all hoped Maso would not be one of them.

As we walked, the blare of sirens from several fire engines in the distance startled us. White smoke rose above the buildings a few blocks away in the general vicinity of our home. We hurried along, joining a growing crowd of people running in the same direction.

Rounding the corner, we saw the smoke billowing from our apartment building. I would find out later that Mom's fears had been realized. The defective wiring had created an electrical short, and something had caught on fire, spreading quickly through the apartment.

No one got hurt in the blaze. Guiso and I ran to Mom and Dad who were standing on the sidewalk in a state of shock. Benjy was with them. I don't know where the rest of my brothers and sisters were. Had the fire started at night when we were asleep, the results would have been even more disastrous.

Mom never stopped believing that the landlord, without any regard for the lives of the tenants, had deliberately started the fire to collect insurance money. Though I didn't think of it at the time, the fire may have been a blessing in disguise. When you go through a catastrophic event, you quickly learn to appreciate the value of human life, especially those you love. It is one of life's reality checks. Now, we were out on the street. But we still had each other and our growing number of relatives in East Chicago could be depended upon to give us food and shelter until Dad could find another place for us to live.

One of those relatives was my *padrino* (godfather), Mom's older brother, Luis, who I had been named after. He dropped by for a visit after we found a new place to live. "New place" is a relative term, I suppose, as Mom hung sheets around the apartment to serve as walls, and all the tenants had to use one bathroom at the end of a dark hallway.

Tío Luis called me over to him. "*Ven acá, muchacho.*" I walked over to him obediently. "Your mother tells me you're having a birthday in a few days, is that right?"

"*Sí, tío,*" I replied. I indicated the number of years by raising seven fingers."

Tío Luis nodded and pulled some cash out of his pocket. My eyes grew as big as saucers as he peeled off a five-dollar bill and handed it to me.

Mine weren't the only eyes that were growing big. While the adults returned to their grown-up conversation, Maso pulled me aside and spoke to me in a confidential tone of voice.

"Luisito, you wanna' go see a movie?"

"A movie? Really?" I said breathlessly. Maso knew how much I wanted to go to a movie theater. It would be my first time.

"We'll get you some candy," he said.

"A Coke and popcorn, too?"

"Whatever you want," said Maso.

"I'll tell Ma," I said, starting toward the living room.

But Maso stopped me. "Nah, don't do that."

Why?"

"She's busy right now. She'll get mad and she won't want you spending your birthday money on candy."

"Or a movie?"

"That, too."

I nodded. "Yeah ..."

"We'll just keep it a secret between you and me. *¿Está bien?*"

I nodded enthusiastically. When the time seemed right, Maso spirited me away from the apartment building. We hurried down the block to the nearest bus stop. Next thing I knew, we were on a bus headed downtown. We got off across the street from a Spanish-language movie theater, and Maso took my money to buy tickets. Then he escorted me inside the dark, air-conditioned theater.

"Candy and soda?" I reminded him, as we passed the refreshment stand.

"Let's find a seat first," said Maso. "Then I'll get you your candy and soda." Maso found me a good seat in the middle of the theater near the front. "I'll be right back," he said.

"Hurry," I urged him.

"You got it."

"¡Cállense!" (Be quiet!) shouted someone in the theater.

I took a final look back at Maso, as he disappeared behind a thick curtain at the back of the theater and, presumably, went to the refreshment stand to buy my birthday goodies. But I quickly forgot all about him. The movie featured the Mexican comedian, Mario Moreno as *Cantinflas,* hilarious as always with his funny pointed hat and baggy pants dangling below his waist. Many people called him the Spanish-speaking Charlie Chaplin, and his antics immediately pulled me into the story.

I was in the theater for hours, how many I don't know, watching the same movie repeatedly, oblivious to the passing of time. When the last showing ended and the screen went black a final time, I looked around and realized I was sitting in the theater all alone. How odd, I thought. Something was wrong. Where was Maso? Why hadn't he come back? I felt scared. The theater was empty, except for me, and spooky in the dark.

After what must have been another five or ten minutes, I gathered enough courage to pry myself from my seat to search for my brother. I reached the lobby and was dismayed to find the refreshment stand closed and the foyer empty. It was already dark outside.

An overwhelming fear seized me, and I began to cry. Maso had abandoned me, and I had no idea how to get home. What would I do? I looked up at the mute faces of box office stars María Felix and Pedro Armandáriz staring back at me from the movie poster of the Mexican film *La Escondida* ("The Hidden One"). The title seemed oddly ironic, as I, too, was hidden and had no idea how to get out of my dilemma.

I pushed on the bar that unlocked the door leading out to the street and stepped onto the sidewalk. Bright car lights flashed and sped by. I had no idea how to get home. I headed off in the direction I thought made the most sense. I don't know how far I walked or how much time passed, but after a while I came across a passageway that looked familiar. I walked down the passageway and knocked on the first door I came to. Miraculously, it turned out to be Tío Luis' apartment. He looked down at me in disbelief. I was overjoyed to see him, but that happiness was not reciprocated.

"¿*Muchacho, que haces tú aquí?*" (What're you doing here, boy?) he said sternly. "Everybody's worried sick about you! Where've you been?"

I tried to explain what had happened, how Maso had left me in the theater, but I was too tired and traumatized to get the words out properly. Exasperated and impatient, Tío Luis tossed his hands in the air. He found his car keys, then bundled me into his old Ford and drove me the rest of the way home.

"Tu papá te va a dar una pela cuando llegues a tu casa." ("Your dad's gonna give you a spanking when you get home.")

The threat was all I heard, and my anxiety grew. But I knew that couldn't be right. Dad wouldn't punish me. I had done nothing wrong! Maso had taken me to the movies, then he had taken my birthday money and abandoned me. Surely, Dad would understand. I would politely ask Dad for his *bendición* (blessing), a sign of respect young Puerto Ricans showed their elders, especially their parents. Mom would fix me a bowl of *sopa* (soup), and I'd sleep away the terror and exhaustion. Everything would be all right.

When I got home, I shouted "¡*Papi!*" and ran to Dad. It was like running into a brick wall. He didn't throw his arms around me. He didn't check to see if I was all right. He didn't ask me to explain what had happened.

As I humbly asked for his *bendición*, he pointed to Mom in the corner, her eyes red from crying, and yanked off his belt. Then he turned me around and began to spank me. It seemed like it would never stop. I gritted my teeth, not wanting him to see me cry. My efforts at *machismo* ("manliness") didn't last long before I was broken. Finally, he stopped and sent me to bed. From that day on, my relationship with Dad, Tío Luis, and Maso was never quite the same.

Chapter 7

STRETCHING MY WINGS

Back in those days, or at least in my neighborhood in East Chicago, parents didn't typically give their children allowances. Heck, it was hard enough to get a nickel for the candy apples sold at school fundraisers! When I saw other kids my age hustling for money after school and on weekends, I wanted to do the same. Mom was concerned about my being so young and walking the streets, but she wasn't opposed to the idea of my earning some money if it was done honestly. Finally, I gained permission to try my hand earning a few dollars out in the world.

One of the conditions was that I had to be accompanied by Guiso on our exploits. I think it gave Mom a sense of security to know my older half-brother was keeping an eye on me.

Guiso and I started off selling the local Spanish-language newspaper for five cents a copy, making two cents profit from every paper sold. We shaved ice and sold snow cones for five cents each. We didn't do too well because we ate most of our profits.

Before long, I graduated to shoeshine boy. I decided that's where I could make real money. Every weekend, with or without Guiso, I'd apply my trade at the bars and seedy hotels near my neighborhood. I had to be careful. Sometimes my clients would try to walk off without paying me.

Fortunately, there always seemed to be several nice ladies hanging around the men. A lot of them were real pretty, too! They had a way of coaxing the men saying, "Help the kid out and let him give you a shine." Maybe it had to do with the way they looked at the guys, or the way they smiled, but whatever the source of their influence over the men, they saw to it that I got a lot of business. And boy, how they'd complain in front of everybody if I wasn't paid at least the customary fifteen cents a shoeshine! If the customer tried to walk off without paying me, God have mercy on him, because he would never recuperate from the onslaught of choice words directed at him by the ladies.

Mom couldn't help but look at me suspiciously when I'd come home before dinner with ten or more dollars in my pocket to give her. She wondered if I had done something wrong to earn that much money. She had a hard time believing I had earned it from shining shoes at the places where the nice ladies worked.

Even with success, however, there were temptations to take shortcuts. One Saturday morning when I noticed I had run out of shoe polish and had little money in my pocket to buy a new can, I walked into a downtown discount store knowing in advance what I was going to do. You know the old metaphor; an angel sat on one shoulder telling me to heed my mother's advice and never steal, and a devil sat on the other side telling me to steal the can of shoe polish for the greater good. After all, who would miss a little can of shoe polish?

I battled fiercely my conscience as I walked back and forth in front of those shiny new cans all lined up neatly in their individual rows by color. Any trained eye could see what was about to happen.

Finally, when one of the cans happened to find its way into my shoeshine box, a hand reached out from behind and grabbed me by the neck. I turned and looked into the face of an irate store clerk who, even if I had not been caught shoplifting, would have terrified me with her piercing eyes and crooked teeth. She dragged me by the ear to a hidden security office.

Only one thought consumed me—how terribly disappointed my mother would be when she found out her son had been arrested for shoplifting.

After I was questioned and fingerprinted in the back room, the soft-spoken, red-headed store manager walked me out of the store. I thought a police car would be waiting for me at the curb. Instead, as I stepped into the sunlight, he leaned down and gave me some sincere advice.

"Son, no matter how hard things get, you don't have to steal. There's always someone willing to help, if you'll only ask."

He then pulled a crumpled dollar bill out of his pants pocket and told me to go buy the shoe polish I needed and to never steal again.

"Do you understand?" he asked me.

"Yes, sir!" I started to walk away, and then turned back to the manager. "Can I buy it here?"

"You'd better go to the drugstore down the street. Our clerk may still have it out for you."

I walked to the corner drugstore and bought the can of polish. Though tempted to tell Mom about the nice red-headed store manager who had given me a dollar bill, I feared that confession might lead to unwelcome questions. So, I kept my mouth shut.

Nonetheless, I decided to take that store manager's advice and do things the right way in the future.

"There's always someone willing to help you if you will only ask," he had said.

Sure enough, it didn't take long before I met someone who fit that description.

Joe Kopack drove throughout East Chicago and the surrounding towns selling fruits and vegetables from the back of a big box truck. I had seen him before in the neighborhood when he parked by the pedestrian bridge near the steel mill and sold to the workers as they headed home after a long day's work. Something told me to approach him and ask him to give me and Guiso jobs.

He was a balding man, and he looked down at me from what seemed a dizzying height.

"I can't hire you, kid."

"Why not, sir?"

"Well, you're underage for one thing. How old are you?"

"I'm eight."

"See what I mean?"

"But I'm a hard worker, sir."

Mr. Kopack gave me and Guiso each an apple and told us to run along. But I wasn't one to give up that easily.

"Get your oranges and apples here, folks!" I sang spontaneously, holding up my apple as I performed an impromptu dance for the people walking by. "Two dollars for a crate. Won't find a better rate! Apples and oranges, before it's too late!"

Mr. Kopack broke into a hearty laugh. Several people had stopped to watch my little show, and one of them bought some fruits and vegetables. As Mr. Kopack gave the steelworker his change, I sang the song again and another man stopped. He bought a box of tomatoes! Mr. Kopack started getting busy with customers and peeked over at me a few times. He made a circular motion with his hand, signaling me to keep singing. I had won him over!

"Okay, little guy," he said a half hour later. "I'll give you some work to do. But I'm not hiring you. It's against the law."

"Then what're you gonna have us do?" I asked.

"Just do your little song and dance routine. People seem to like it. I'll give you fruits and vegetables at the end of the day that, uh, have gone a little bit ripe. Don't worry. When I first started out, that's how I fed my family. You just cut off the bad parts and you'll have plenty left over."

"And you'll hire my brother, too?"

"This is your brother?" asked Mr. Kopack, looking Guiso up and down.

"Yes, sir."

"Okay. He looks strong enough. He can help me load and unload the truck. But the same deal goes for him, too. This is all off the books."

And that is how Guiso and I started to work for Mr. Kopack. Sure, I would have preferred to be paid in cash, but I didn't complain. I enjoyed the work and it made my parents happy.

One day, after I had been working for Mr. Kopack for about two months, Guiso and I were riding in the open back of the truck. I somehow lost my balance and was hurled headlong into the street. I was knocked unconscious by the fall and rushed to a hospital. A day later I woke up at home with a splitting headache. Mom was leaning over me and crying. When she saw me coming to, she squeezed my hands and started to shout. Dad appeared alongside her. He looked every bit as worried as she did.

"Ben... di... ción..." I said to my dad weakly, requesting a blessing.

"*Dios te bendiga, hijo,*" he replied softly. ("God bless you.")

A third person appeared between Mom and Dad, Abuela Enriqueta, Dad's mother. She had arrived a few weeks earlier from Puerto Rico. She touched my bandaged head and cradled my jaw in her hand.

"Be careful! Don't hurt him," protested Mom.

Abuela took her hand from my chin and examined other parts of my body.

"He needs to rest," Mom said. "Let's leave him alone."

"This *muchacho* needs a cold washcloth on his head right now," said Abuela, touching my forehead. "He's got a fever."

"I'm taking him back to the hospital," said Mom. "My brother is coming to pick us up."

"He doesn't need a doctor!" said Abuela. "I have experience with these things, you know. Please! Bring me a wet cloth."

Mom's eyes turned to my dad.

"What's wrong, *mi amor*? She's only trying to help."

"*Hay muchos caciques y pocos indios aqui,*" shouted Mom, walking away in frustration. ("There are many chiefs and not enough Indians here.")

I squeezed my eyes shut. The noise was making my pain worse. I smelled something strong and opened my eyes. Abuela Enriqueta was only inches from my face. She grinned and began rubbing the part of my forehead that wasn't bandaged with alcohol. From a corner of the room, Dad loudly hummed his rendition of *El Lamento Borincano*, as though wanting to drown out Mom's ramblings in the kitchen.

Gradually, I recovered from my injuries and went back to work for Mr. Kopack. From that time on, he treated me differently, as if I

70

were someone special. He bought me a white shirt, a black satin jacket, and a nice pair of black pants. He even promised to take me to a Chicago White Sox game.

I could hardly sleep the night before the game. We went to Comiskey Park on a warm and sunny Wednesday afternoon. There before me on the baseball field were the likes of Luis Aparicio and none other than left-handed hitter, Jim Rivera, a Puerto Rican. He was what we call a Nuyorican because he had been born in New York City to Puerto Rican parents.

I thought I had died and gone to heaven! I looked around the big stadium, at the thousands of cheering fans and the chalky-white baseball diamond against the immaculate dark green grass. Mr. Kopack bought me a soft drink and a hot dog with mustard and the game started.

My eyes were on Rivera constantly. My brother Vitín had told me stories about how Rivera was one of the most popular players on the White Sox team, because of the reckless abandon with which he played the game. He had earned the nickname "Jungle Jim" from a Chicago sportswriter for his speed and the way he'd dive head first into the bases.

When the six-footer stole third base with a wild slide on his stomach, the fans went wild.

I jumped to my feet along with everyone else and shouted, "Hooray for Rivera! My brother is Jim Rivera, too!" Back in Puerto Rico,

Vitín had been given that nickname when he played baseball with his friends.

Mr. Kopack couldn't have been nicer that day. When he drove me home after the game, he asked me if my parents were doing okay.

"They're fine," I said.

"Listen, Louie," he said to me. "I just want you to know that I'm really sorry about the accident."

"The accident?"

"You know, when you fell off my truck."

"Oh, that was a long time ago, Mr. Kopack. I'm okay now."

"Yeah, well ... that's good. That's good. You're a nice kid and all."

"Thanks, Mr. Kopack."

Mr. Kopack nodded. For some reason, he still looked worried. My parents were aware that they could have sued for an undetermined amount of money, but it wasn't how we treated those that had been good to us. After all, he was my boss. I smiled at him, and he smiled back.

A week or so later, after talking with my dad, Mr. Kopack offered to rent us a house he owned in nearby Gary, Indiana, at a reduced rent. We were desperate for a bigger place and Dad agreed. But even with the projected move, Mom and Abuela Enriqueta continued to have friction. Grandma was respectful and loving, but, like my mom, she had a strong take-charge character and was very protective of my dad.

As for Dad, he was seldom home. One night, I asked Mom why.

"He is busy with his friends," she said and cut the conversation short, chopping *cilantro* and onions to add to the *sofrito* she was making.

I had never seen her look so sad. Her eyes watered, and I didn't know if it was because of the onions or Dad visiting his friends.

Mom started to cry. Benjy, who was playing with metal bottlecaps, went to her and hugged her legs. She picked him up, and he kissed her cheek, then wiped away her tears with his little hands. Mom really lost it then. She held on to the two of us like she was in a dark ocean and we were lifelines someone had thrown overboard for her to hang onto.

"I just want the two of you to do something good with your lives," she said through her tears. "I want you to get an education and get a good office job. Both of you. Will you do that for me, *mis hijos*." ("my sons")

Benjy nodded solemnly, and I squeezed Mom's hands as tight as I could. "Things are good, Ma," I said. "We're moving into a nice neighborhood."

"And a big house!" chimed in Benjy.

"Things will get better," I said. And I was sure they would. I believed in my family's tenacity and the American Dream.

LIVING BETWEEN CULTURES

Chapter 8

BROKEN FAMILY

Material things can certainly make a person's life more enjoyable, but it's also true that possessions alone cannot buy happiness. The house in Gary was nicer than anything we had ever known as a family, but it didn't reduce tensions between Mom and Dad.

We had only been there a few months when Mom made the final decision to divorce Dad. It wasn't just his penchant for "being busy with his friends." According to Mom, he didn't place the same value on the education of his children as she did. He didn't share the same vision for the family's future, which translated in her mind as a promise of failure for me and Benjy.

Mom had never finished grade school and she rightly saw that the path to success in the "Land of Opportunity" was to get a good education. As she was fond of saying, a good education was something no one could take away from us, something that would serve us well the rest of our lives.

In fairness to Dad, rarely did anyone have a disparaging word to say about him. He was a likable person and unafraid of hard work. But he was at heart a *Jibarito,* a worker of the earth who saw life in humble and basic terms. He knew survival could be achieved by your own hard labor. In our case, acquiring an advanced education would be left to the individual, to one's own initiative.

The arguments between my parents intensified. Mom wanted more, and she felt it was always two against one. Abuela Enriqueta could be counted on to be protective of her son and support him even though she didn't always agree with my father's actions.

One morning, Mom packed her suitcase and told me and Benjy she was going to the Bronx in New York City to stay with her cousin, Ramonita. When I asked her why, she said she and Dad were getting a divorce.

"I'll come back for you as soon as I can," she promised.

While our parents had agreed on the separation arrangements, the news devastated

Benjy and me, knowing that my mother would leave us for an unknown period. How could she walk away from us and how could my father agree to it? We cried, but I cried the least because I knew I needed to comfort Benjy as best I could.

For weeks after Mom left, we had trouble sleeping. Eventually, we adjusted to her absence with the hope we would see her return at any minute. At least the arguments between her and Dad became a faint memory. Abuela took over raising us, and I had my schoolwork and part-time jobs to keep me busy.

Meanwhile, in the Bronx, Ramonita's husband, Max, worked as a barber and knew almost everyone in the Puerto Rican community in and around Third Avenue and East 149th Street. Max helped Mom get a job as a cook at a nearby restaurant. While working there, Mom met a tall, handsome man named Tito, as his friends called him. Tito had been recently divorced and was raising two school-age daughters on his own. Mom, along with a lot of other women, found his good looks and dedication to his daughters overwhelmingly attractive.

After getting to know each other, Mom accepted Tito's invitation to become his common-law wife. A few months later, the two of them came to Indiana, intent on taking Benjy and me to live with them in the Bronx. They stayed with Mom's younger brother, Tommy, who lived in Chicago.

Uncle Tommy had always gotten along well with Dad and was able to serve as a mediator between Dad and Mom. But when Mom asked to take me and Benjy with her, Dad objected. Benjy, the youngest, was his favorite. No surprise there. I could go, but not the "baby." In the end, Mom and Tito left with me in tow until Mom could convince Dad to let her have Benjy, too.

I was nervous and excited all at once. I looked forward to living with Mom again, but I worried about leaving Benjy behind, even if I was jealous of all the attention he got. My relationship with Dad was strained by this point. The previous months, even with Mom out of the picture, had done very little to draw us closer. I had so many unanswered questions. What had happened to the love between him and Mom? Why didn't he spend personal time with me or show me any fatherly affection?

The day before I was to leave with Mom, I decided I'd tell Dad goodbye. It was a Saturday morning, and he was off from work. I could hear him moving around in his bedroom, so I knocked on the door.

"*¿Quién es?*" ("Who is it?")

"It's me, Luis."

"Come in."

I softly pushed the door open and peered into the room. Dad sat on a chair tying his shoes. He tilted his head up to look at me. Our conversation was in Spanish.

"I just ... I just ..." I couldn't seem to finish the sentence. Dad stood and went to his dresser. He put on his watch and glanced over at me.

"So, you are leaving tomorrow?"

"Yes."

Dad nodded. "Are you sure you want to go?"

"I want to be with Mom."

Dad turned and looked me full in the face. "I can understand that."

"But I ... I don't want to leave Benjy behind."

"Benjy's staying with me."

"I know."

"Okay, well ... Anyway, I need to go out."

"Where are you going?"

Dad put a money clip in his pocket and observed me a while in silence. "You don't need to know where I'm going, but I'll tell you. I'm going over to Guthrie Street to play dominoes with Raúl and the guys. You want to come?"

The invitation took me by surprise since I hadn't been anywhere with Dad for months. You'd have thought I would jump at the chance to do something with him. But I didn't.

"That's kind of far. I probably need to stay here. Uncle Tommy's coming later to pick me up."

Dad walked by me, patting me once on the head. "That's fine." Then he leaned over and gave me a quick hug and continued into the hallway, turning once. With a quivering voice he said, "Be safe in *Nueva* York."

The door shut behind him, and I hurried over to the peephole to see outside. I caught a glimpse of him through the fogged glass as he walked away. An impulse to throw open the door and run after him came over me. But what good would that have done? It would only postpone the inevitable.

Chapter 9

THE THIRD WHEEL

I spent nearly two years living in the Bronx with Mom, Tito, and his two daughters. The youngest, Nancy, was a year or two younger than Benjy. Sophia, the oldest, was my age.

It was not a happy time. I thought I'd be the recipient of Mom's affections again, but it was my stepfather and two stepsisters who seemed to get all the attention. I was the third wheel around our home, the outsider. School was a challenge for me, too. I had a hard time concentrating on my studies and didn't have many friends. I have no doubt, underneath it all, lingered the trauma of my parents' divorce and the dismantling of our family.

I would often sneak up to the roof of the apartment building in the late afternoons or at night and lean over the roof's edge to gaze on the massive spread of the city. We lived on East 179th and Webster Avenue, between the heavily transited Grand Concourse and Third Avenue. In the relative quiet of my rooftop perch, I felt isolated from the tumult of the world. The relentless noise of the city seemed far away, and a measure of peace flooded my soul at least for a little while.

Mom, on the other hand, seemed to become accustomed to her new life when she wasn't thinking about Benjy. After all she had been through, who could begrudge her a little happiness?

Ramona and Max were at the center of a vibrant Latino social life and constantly invited Mom and Tito with them to visit friends or to a big party in one of the nearby boroughs. As a result, I came to learn firsthand how seriously most "Nuyoricans" regarded their clothing and physical appearance. Women, especially Ramonita, dressed like Broadway starlets with elegant dresses and bouffant hairstyles. The men wore expensive suits and fedoras. Every hair on their heads and moustaches was neatly trimmed and slicked back in place. By comparison, in the steel town where I had come from in the Midwest, most Latinos dressed more modestly.

My mother had always been a beautiful woman, but when she went out for the evening—

wow! Good thing Tito was big and strong. No one chased after her with him around.

One day while I was riding with Tito, an accident happened ahead of us. One driver was pinned inside his car. Several men tried to open the door, but it wouldn't budge. Tito told the men to step back, and he literally ripped the car door off its hinges. I never gave Tito any problems after that. Mom and I were living with a superman!

Tito could also be a lot of fun. Another day, while riding with him, Mom, and some other grownups, we saw Bobby Capó walking along Third Avenue. Tito honked the horn, and everyone waved at Mr. Capó from the car. Everyone, except me.

With the window rolled down I asked innocently, "Who's Bobby Capó?" not knowing he could hear me.

Mr. Capó was a superstar to his compatriots as a great vocalist-songwriter and Spanish language radio and television celebrity.

Tito swerved into a parking space, and we piled out of the car. In short order, I found myself standing in front of Puerto Rico's beloved son and singing legend who, after listening to Tito carry on for a few seconds, bent down to address me. "So, you don't know who Bobby Capó is?" he asked with a smile.

I shook my head.

"Forgive him, Mr. Capó," interjected Tito. "I'll take him home and play all your records for him. I have every one of them!"

Mr. Capó laughed good-naturedly and sang a few bars from *Me Lo Dijo Adela*, which had a nice cha-cha rhythm. With the grown-ups encouraging me, I showed off a few of my dance moves and won an even bigger smile from Mr. Capó. When he continued on his way, we piled back in the car and followed him for a while, honking the horn and waving excitedly.

Around this time, Tito got a better paying job working for a cabinet-making company, and Mom stayed home to care for the children. One morning, Tito's ex-wife and a male companion came by the apartment to see Nancy and Sophia. Mom wouldn't let them through the door; she was afraid they had come to take the girls away while Tito was at work.

"Come back later when Tito's here," she told them through the half-open door.

The guy started making threats. He was well dressed and acted like a bigshot. "You have to let us see them *now*," he insisted.

"I don't have to do nothing," said Mom defiantly, and shut the door in their faces.

After a few moments, we heard their footsteps going down the stairwell. Probably an hour passed when there was another knock at the door. They were back, insisting that Mom let them in to see the girls. By this time, I was fully alerted to the situation and stood behind Mom brandishing the only weapon I could find, a butter knife.

"Don't worry, Mom, I'll protect you!" I shouted in my best tough-guy voice. "I got me a knife!"

The argument between Mom and the man at the door grew more intense. Mom suddenly leaned back and punched him square in the eye with all the strength she had. He stumbled backward and fell halfway down the stairs.

"I'm goin' for the *policia!*" he shouted, getting to his feet and hurrying from the apartment building with the woman.

After a half hour or so, they were back with one of New York's finest—a rosy-faced Irishman with blue eyes and a New York City Police Department badge pinned to his jacket.

He calmly listened to both sides of the story and, after staring for a moment at the man's black and blue eye, said, "Looks to me like you threatened her and she was protecting her household."

The couple protested angrily as the officer escorted them down the stairs. It was finished. Mom and I had won the day and successfully protected the damsels in distress. From that time on I was a fan of the NYPD.

Over time, I began to think this second home might just work out after all. And maybe it would have. Tito and Mom did seem to care a lot for each other, and Mom gave everything she had to be a mother to his two daughters. But there were issues just under the surface that threatened to sabotage our blended family.

Tito's mood swings scared me at first. He could be up one moment and down the next. When he cut himself with an electric table saw at work, nearly losing several fingers in the process, he was forced to go on disability. He sank deeper and deeper into depression. Arguments about finances and how to keep the family together became more and more turbulent.

Eventually, Mom decided that separation was the best recourse. She looked for support among her immediate family. By this time, she had a sister as well as more distant relatives living in Hartford, Connecticut, about a hundred miles to the northeast. After going there for a weekend visit with Ramonita and Max, she decided Hartford would become our new home. But first was the matter of getting Benjy back under her wing.

Chapter 10

BORICUA REBIRTH

One of my fondest memories is riding the 20th Century Limited train from New York to Chicago with Mom. Snuggled up close to her, we only took up one seat. It was an express train, and we made the trip in a little over fifteen hours. This time, Dad didn't put up any arguments and allowed Mom to take Benjy. His main support, Abuela Enriqueta, worn out from all the household duties and looking after Benjy, had returned to Puerto Rico. Dad, to his credit, realized he had to let Benjy go for the sake of love. He knew it was the right thing to do.

Reunited with my little brother, Mom sat the two of us down at Uncle Tommy's place in Chicago and explained her plan. Benjy and I would go to Puerto Rico for six or seven months to stay with our maternal grandparents, while she went to Hartford to find a job and a place for us to live. Then she would send for us, meet us at the airport, and take us to our new home in Connecticut. We were going to be with our mom once again! Not only that, I was going to return to the place of my birth, *Borinquen,* the Enchanted Isle across the sea. Uncle Tommy put on a *Cortijo y Su Combo* record, and we all danced.

Benjy and I flew out of Midway Airport in August 1961, destination San Juan with an intermediate stop in New York. As two boys traveling alone, we received extra care and attention from the airline personnel. On the ground in San Juan, an airline representative double-checked the identification card of the taxi driver, a family friend who had been sent to pick us up in his *carro público.*

As we stepped from the arrival area onto the sidewalk, a multitude of sensations hit us all at once. The air was much warmer and more humid than I had expected. We could hear people around us talking in all kinds of languages, Spanish and English of course, but other languages, too. We loaded our bags into the *carro público* and rode for what seemed like several hours to the south-central coast of the island.

We finally arrived in Santa Isabel and made our way to the *Felicia Primera* neighborhood where our grandparents lived.

What a joy to see our *abuelos* and enjoy a delicious, home-cooked meal!

"Now, it's time to go to bed," said Abuela Eugeñia, not long after dinner was finished, and the dishes washed and put away.

I wasn't used to going to bed so early but was happy to oblige.

Geña, as she was called, escorted us to our cramped bedroom where a *mosquitero* (mosquito net) hung from the four corner-posts of a bed. Benjy and I had no idea what the *mosquitero* was for. After Grandma Geña explained its function and kissed us goodnight, Benjy and I scrambled under the netting and stared up at the zinc corrugated metal roof through the sheer-white material of the fabric. The light around us diffused. It seemed as if we were in another world. It wasn't long before we pretended to be pirates on the Caribbean Sea or Native American Indians sitting in our own teepee, or anything else that struck our fancy.

Rounding out the novelty of our new dwelling were the harmless *legartijos* (little brownish-green lizards) crawling along the walls and rafters. Over time, they became our pets, and we looked forward to seeing and playing with them.

When I woke up early the next morning needing to use the bathroom, Abuelo Anfiloquío ("Filoquío" for short) pointed me in the direction of the *letrina,* a narrow, one-person outhouse in the back yard. I stepped gingerly across the yard. It would be several weeks before my bare feet would adjust to the Puerto Rican soil and sand. I opened the door to the *letrina* and, staring me in the face, was a wooden box-seat with a hole in the center. The odor wafting from below almost made me lose my breath. I did my business quickly and made a speedy exit.

In addition to the insects and small creatures that called the *letrina* home, several large frogs croaked loudly and hopped around in the mess underneath. It was one more thing to get used to. But when you're young, everything is an adventure. You learn to adapt quickly.

It was a time of innocence and an opportunity for new experiences, somewhat different from the roles we took on living and playing in the alleyways up north, where we were forced to become little men and women in children's bodies. It soon became normal not to see traffic jams or walk past skyscrapers or high-rise apartment buildings. There were no neon lights at night or rushing subway trains. Everything a person needed was close by, starting with the juicy mangos and *aguacates* (avocados) that grew abundantly in every family's yard.

I was amazed how fruits and vegetables grew everywhere. With the combination of warm sun and humidity, everything seemed to sprout from the ground. Back in the States, people would wait in great anticipation for family or friends to return from the island with a care package of these delicacies. Here, in this fertile island, bags full of produce would be shared with family and friends, the rest left to rot on the ground.

We never went hungry. There was poverty in Santa Isabel, yes, but it didn't seem to cause people to steal or harm others or take drugs. On the contrary, folks seemed accustomed to sharing their food with one another. It was common for a neighbor to drop in to see Abuela Geña and give her a few eggs or vegetables and for Geña to do the same.

A bustling entrepreneurial spirit thrived on the island. I enjoyed watching the street vendors push their food carts down the dusty streets or ride by slowly on bicycles. One old man daily carried a basket of freshly baked *pan de agua* or *pan de manteca* on his bicycle handlebars, singing as he went along.

Abuelo Filoquío was a foreman in the sugarcane fields. Soft-spoken and dignified-looking with white hair and fair skin, he was a living portrait of his Spanish ancestors. By contrast, Geña was lightly tanned with darker hair like a native Taina Indian woman. Among her many attributes, she was an excellent cook. Tall and slender, she kept her long, graying hair tied in a bun. Though stricter than

Abuelo, she had trouble keeping a straight face when it came time to discipline us. Benjy and I were little comedians who specialized in getting people to laugh.

As soon as we saw that Grandma was upset about something we had done, we'd go to work on her before she had time to figure out an appropriate punishment. We'd perform little dances or voice imitations and gestures of family members. Before long, she would cover her mouth to keep us from seeing her smile. She'd make a show of stomping her foot and sending us from the room in mock anger. Benjy and I would leave dutifully, looking contrite, and then linger by the doorway as she began to laugh and say something to herself like, "*Nenes traviesos. ¡Como los amo!*" ("Mischievous kids. How I love them!")

For me and Benjy, our *abuelos* were a refuge from the emotional storms we had been through in the States, and we grew to love them dearly. They had the patience to humor our boyish antics, and it was a healing balm for us to be around them day and night.

I grew especially close to Abuelo Filoquío, not only because he would come home every day with sweet sugarcane cuttings, but because of his humble and gentle demeanor. When not in school, one of my chores was to go into the sugarcane fields before noon and take him a triple stack of round, white-enameled lunch pails that separated the rice, beans, and meat (when the latter was available). I couldn't understand why he would want to eat such a heavy lunch when back in the States many working people settled for a sandwich or hot dogs and hamburgers.

On his days off, when I least expected it, Abuelo Filoquío would sneak me out of the house and take me to a small, corner kiosk where I would cool off with a *piragua* (snow cone). I loved watching the *piraguero* scrape the top of the ice block with his handheld metal shaver and drop the shavings into a white paper cone. Then he would pour a mixture of strawberry and *tamarindo* syrup topped with honey over the ice and hand it to me with a smile. That was the real deal. No imitation flavors there!

I would savor each mouthful of flavored ice on my tongue for as long as possible. Meanwhile, Abuelo stood nearby and nibbled on a piece of *mortadella* and a couple of soda crackers while nursing a cold drink. Not a worry in the world.

Two of my aunts and a younger male cousin also lived at our grandparents' home. Both of my aunts were still in high school and our little cousin, Luisito, was too young to attend school. He was almost three years old and was the whitest little Puerto Rican Benjy and I had ever seen. With golden curls bouncing as he ran, he spent most of his time playing with the family dog named Chee-leen, a mixed breed (*Sato*) that resembled a lean Australian dingo.

The younger of the two aunts, Carmen, had native Taino Indian features and a golden bronze complexion, while Dina and Luisito could have been mistaken for blue-eyed Scandinavians. Puerto Rico is a "rainbow nation" of different ancestries and colors, even in the same family, and we were the perfect example of what it is to be *Puertorriqueños*!

Dina and Carmen helped me and Benjy with our homework (which was in Spanish, of course). They'd also defend us on the Brumbaugh Elementary School playground if kids picked on us or made fun of our gringo accents.

My aunts did something that had a profound impact on me. They greeted Abuelo at the end of each workday when he came home covered in the dust and grime of the sugarcane fields. Our aunts filled a white enamel basin with water, knelt in front of him, and gently took off his boots. With loving care, they washed his feet while he sat there immobile, drained of energy. Then they lifted his feet and dried them with a towel.

In our naiveté Benjy and I didn't think this was a chore we wanted to do. We never volunteered to do it, but as an adult I often recall this act as an example of great love and reverence demonstrated by my aunts, Carmen and Dina, for their father.

There's a saying that all good things must come to an end, and so it was with our stay in paradise. Seven months passed and Mom had settled in Hartford. The time came to rejoin her in the States. Hugging my grandparents and saying goodbye, something told me I'd return to Borinquen one day.

I had my mother's drive to succeed in life and could only imagine where that might take me, but I had something from my father, too; something simple, yet profound. Like him, I was a *jíbaro*, a country boy. I was loyal, culturally and otherwise to my new home, but I knew I would never be far from the island of my birth. Puerto Rico would ever be in my waking moments and in my dreams.

Chapter 11

REUNITED

After the long plane ride, I couldn't have been happier to see Mom at LaGuardia Airport when she suddenly emerged from the crowd with a shout and a flashing smile. Her excitement at having her little men back with her was evident; she couldn't stop hugging Benjy and me.

We sang Mom a duet in the car as we drove to our new home in Hartford. We had heard the song on the island's radio, and our rendition made Mom laugh so hard tears rolled down her cheeks.

Good times were ahead for sure. Watching Mom's happy tears, I pulled Benjy to my side in a playful embrace.

In the early 1960s, Hartford looked like any other racially diverse New England city. The Puerto Rican community was the predominant Latino group in town, with a large percentage of people who, like my father, had come to the mainland as migrant farm workers and had later moved on to various American cities in search of new opportunities.

As has always been true of immigrants, most of these Latino blue-collar workers settled in neighborhoods where our people congregated and where they could afford the rent. That meant they could end up living in buildings owned by slum landlords that had been vacated during periods of white flight. Most Caucasian families moved out once they saw the neighborhood turning brown.

It seemed to bother some people that many of us lived together under one roof. I suppose this was just one of many differences in our cultures. Latinos preferred living among their extended family and within a close community of friends. Our neighborhoods became the centers of our activities and everyone knew each other. This meant that *bochinche* (gossip) was pervasive, joys and sorrows were shared, and any adult had the right to twist the ear of someone else's child who was getting out of line.

I loved stepping off the sidewalk into our apartment building and breathing in the mouthwatering scents of *arroz con pollo* (yellow rice with chicken) or the succulent pork chops seasoned with *adobo*, simmering in the *caserolas* (cooking pots) of a half-dozen different Puerto Rican households.

While the grownups in our neighborhood worked hard to stretch their meager incomes and pay the monthly bills, youngsters like me were more often found on the street corners telling tall tales or posturing for leadership. I would soon be turning thirteen years old, my season for coming of age.

My neighborhood friends had nicknames like *Gol-dee-locks, Marcelino-Pan-y-Vino*, and *Elvi* (short for Elvis). Along with the street corners, we explored every square inch of our block on South Main Street.

Our favorite hangout was 280 Main Street, where Benjy and I lived with Mom in an efficiency apartment on the second floor. Boys and girls were introduced to their first kisses on the back wooden stairway of the three-story building. They talked about their favorite Motown music and the new British band, the Beatles, who appeared on TV's Ed Sullivan Show. During the hot summer afternoons and evenings, tenants talked across their porches about the local gossip or the latest news from Puerto Rico.

We all stayed within the neighborhood, which provided a sense of community. Most of the time, we shared a peaceful existence. But there were also moments when a family argument spilling out into a hallway or down the stairs shattered the peace. Such *discusiones* (arguments) quickly became everyone's business. After words or slaps were exchanged, the problem was usually settled, and life returned to what was considered normal.

As we had done in Indiana, Benjy, Mom, and I all slept in one bedroom. Money was tight and so was space in our small apartment. One Saturday morning in early June 1962, I awoke from a disturbing dream concerning Benjy. Though only half-awake, I followed my first instinct and checked on him. He slept peacefully nearby, and I breathed a deep sigh of relief.

Sounds of breakfast being prepared in the kitchenette floated towards me, and I looked over at the clock on the clothes dresser. It was six thirty in the morning, still too early to get up. But I was awake now and could smell the dark roast *Bustelo* coffee brewing. I hoped there was enough cream of wheat left in our small cupboard so Benjy and I could eat something solid.

I loved Saturdays, my favorite day of the week. After finishing my chores, I'd head over to my spot in front of Nelson's Drugstore across the street to set up shop as a shoeshine boy right there on the sidewalk. I almost always did well. I had several years of experience shining shoes and had developed one special trick that became my trademark. For the last polish, I'd take a four-inch wide piece of nylon I had cut from the top of one of Mom's old stockings and skim it hard across the shoe leather. The friction from the nylon warmed the polish so that it melted into the shoe leather and then hardened to a gleaming shine. Sometimes, the customer didn't want to walk away once I had finished for fear the magic might disappear. And I almost never got polish on a man's socks, which was especially important in 1962 when many men wore white socks with their black or brown dress shoes.

The sunny and mild weather brought a booming business this particular Saturday. As the morning wore on, I looked more frequently up the street at St. Simon's Catholic Church. I always did my best to go to the large, ornate stone building on a Saturday to make my confession. I loved the feeling of leaving the noise and glare of the street when I crossed the threshold of the church and entered its dimly lit, calm, and soothing atmosphere. Knowing I'd be safe there, I would let out a big sigh when I entered. In my twelve-year old mind, I thought I was drawing closer to God for a time and showing Him proper respect.

Around noon, I made my way south on Main Street to the church. The intricate stained-glass windows always caught my eye upon entering, as did the flickering votive candles burning here and there. The murmured prayers of a handful of faithful caressed my soul. I took a seat in one of the hard wood pews to soak up the peaceful atmosphere.

My mind drifted to the event planned for later that evening. I had become a Boy Scout and a big awards ceremony was to be held at the Central Baptist Church a few blocks north. I already knew my mother did not plan to attend. She was too tired and too busy. It wouldn't be the first time or the last. Now I needed to make sure Benjy didn't go with me. He'd only be in the way and would probably wander off and get lost when the time came for me to receive my badge.

I entered the confessional booth to clear my accounts with the Man Upstairs.

"Bless me Father for I have sinned," I said to the invisible priest behind the black opaque cloth screen. "It's been a whole week since my last confession and these are my sins." I cleared my throat. "I lied to my mother about the plastic dog."

"The plastic dog?" interrupted the priest.

"She bought a plastic dog to be a ... to be a ... I think she calls it a home decoration or something. But it's really just a toy. She likes to keep it on the dresser and tells us not to touch it without her permission."

"A child should always obey his mother."

"Yes, Father. My little brother plays with it, too. More than I do."

"You're confessing your sins, my son, not those of your brother."

"Yes, Father."

I hesitated before continuing. "And I, uh ... I also got jealous of my brother again." I stopped myself. I wished I had not said "again."

"What happened, my son?"

"Well, we got our report cards back from school."

"Did he get better grades than you?"

I raised my eyebrows. This priest seemed to know what I was going to say before I said it. "Yeah, and then Mom gave him a treat."

"Anything else, my son?"

I cleared my throat gain. "I took some candy out of the drawer where Mom hides it."

"Yes?"

"Without her permission," I mumbled.

"That's stealing, my son."

"Yes, Father, I know. But I'm going to buy some Mary Jane's at the drugstore when I get back to work, and I'll put 'em in Mom's drawer. She'll like that."

"Does she like Mary Jane's?"

"She likes any kind of candy. Just so long as it has a wrapper on it. You know, because of the bugs."

"I understand. Are you going to tell her you took the candy?"

"Should I?"

"The Lord will give you wisdom, my son."

I nodded. My confession complete, the disembodied voice of the priest instructed me to say two Hail Mary's and three Our Fathers and absolved me of my sins.

"Go in peace," he said finally.

I crossed myself with a grateful heart and left the booth. Guilt is a terrible thing to carry around, I thought. But to have your sins forgiven … what a wonderful feeling! I hurried back to the drugstore, worked a couple of hours more, and bought the candy for Mom before heading home.

Chapter 12

SOMETHING UNFORESEEN

It was almost five thirty in the afternoon, and I needed to get going. The Boy Scout award ceremony would be starting in another hour, and I didn't want to be late. But a problem arose. As I had suspected, Benjy wanted to come with me. I pleaded with Mom to let me go alone. After all, how could I be responsible for Benjy if I was going to be called to the front to receive an award?

"He might wander off while I'm standing there," I told Mom. "Who knows where he'll end up? It's a really big church with all kinds of dark rooms and winding hallways. There's a big basement, too. Nobody goes down there."

"Why is that?" asked Mom, her curiosity aroused.

"They say something bad happened down there a long time ago."

"What happened?"

"Well, I don't know the whole story," I said, drawing out my words. Then I added ominously, "But it had to do with ... a spirit."

Mom's eyes widened. She put her arm around Benjy's shoulder and pulled him closer. "He'll stay here. You go by yourself."

"By myself?"

"Benjy's too young. He might wander off."

"Into the basement, you mean."

Mom grabbed Benjy by both shoulders and shook him a little. "Don't you go into no basements, you hear me?"

I looked down at the floor, not wanting Mom to see the slight gleam of satisfaction I was certain would be in my eyes. "There is another option," I said.

"What's that?"

"You could both come. That way, you'll be there with Benjy and he won't wander off to the basement. Almost all the boys will be there with their families."

Mom stood and made her way to the door. "*¡Ay bendito!* Luis. I told you already I can't go! I have to visit your Tía Guilla who is at the hospital. Go to your ceremony and come home right after it ends, okay?"

I nodded. I had kept my expectations low to avoid feeling hurt.

"*Eres un buen muchacho,*" said Mom, telling me I was a good boy. "I need to borrow some coffee from Tía Aurora. Let me know when you're leaving."

Tía Aurora, one of Mom's younger sisters, and her husband Tony lived next door to us in a bigger apartment. Mom liked to spend a lot of time there to keep up with news from Puerto Rico.

Benjy walked over to the clothes dresser and strained to reach the toy dog, a majestic boxer with cropped ears and light brown coloring.

"Benjy, put the dog back," I said.

He raised his big brown eyes and gave me a hurt look. "His name is Brownie," he said.

"Put Brownie back," I said with a sigh. I never knew anyone who could stay angry at Benjy for long, especially my mother. But I loved him, too. He had a way of making people laugh and feel good about themselves. He kissed the plastic dog before I could take it out of his hand. "I tell you what, Ben," I said, placing the dog back on the dresser. "If Mom says it's okay, I'll buy you and me a dog, just like this one."

"A real dog?"

"A real dog!"

"Like Brownie?"

"Like Brownie."

"I'm gonna tell Mom right now!" he exclaimed, running toward the door.

"No, you're not! Stop right where you are! You're gonna stay here like Mom said!"

And with that, I left the apartment. As I shut the door, I heard Benjy back at the dresser, moving things around to get at the plastic dog again. I shook my head, smiling as I imagined how the scenario would play out. Mom would return from Tía Aurora's apartment and find Benjy playing with the dog on the floor. She'd scold him for several seconds, then kiss him and want to feed him something to make him feel better.

I headed down Main Street toward my Scout meeting knowing everything would be all right in the end. Benjy could entertain himself with that dog for hours.

Chapter 13

THE WORLD STOPS

I took my seat on a folding metal chair in the gymnasium of Central Baptist Church and looked around. It didn't feel much like the kind of church I was familiar with. There were no ceramic statues of saints and no burning candles like at Saint Simon's. But what difference did that make? I loved being a Boy Scout and that was enough for me.

Our scoutmaster, Bob Casstevens, who reminded me of a no-nonsense "Hoss" Cartwright in the western television series "Bonanza," gave everyone a warm greeting. He was the biggest and kindest man I had ever seen. As he called us forward individually to receive our new badges, I noticed most of the other kids had family members present to applaud and congratulate them. Tommy Carter's mother repeatedly took pictures of her beaming son with a Polaroid camera. I had no one from my family to share this honor with me.

I thought about my dad, hundreds of miles away in East Chicago, and wondered what he was doing. I pictured him, Mom, and Benjy sitting on the chairs beside me. I had not seen Dad in more than a year. With each passing day, he faded more and more in my memory.

And then, my name was called.

"Louis Ri-ve-ra," intoned Mr. Bob.

I had been baptized "Luis Alberto Rivera Colón," but many *Americanos* found it difficult to say "Lu-ees" or roll their R's in "RRRi-ve-ra."

I strode forward to collect my badge.

Not bad for a twelve-year-old.

I looked over at Tommy Carter's mother just in case she wanted to snap a picture, but she wasn't even clapping. She was changing the film in her camera.

Mr. Bob's deep voice interrupted my thoughts. "This young man has been of great help to me and his fellow scouts. He's always eager to be of service and has demonstrated clear leadership skills. It is our pleasure to present him with ..."

I held my breath as Mr. Bob searched through a large envelope.

"... this First Class badge!" He held up the award for everyone to see.

My hand disappeared inside Mr. Bob's bear-like paw, as he shook my hand and presented me with the round cloth badge. A few people clapped. The smile on Mr. Bob's face made my pre-teen chest swell with pride. At this rate, I'd make Eagle Scout in a couple of years, maybe sooner.

Later, on the way home, I imagined showing my award to Mom and seeing her face light up.

"*¡Que buen muchacho!*" she would exclaim and give me a kiss on the cheek.

Benjy would be there, too, and he'd smile and want to see my badge and give me a hug. And then, less than a block from home, I spotted Lucy, a friend of the family, coming toward me on the other side of the street.

"Luisito! Have you heard!?" she called out.

I looked at her uncomprehendingly.

"Benjy's had an accident," she continued. "Hurry home!"

"Not Benjy!" Surely, it couldn't be true.

But Lucy shouted, "Hurry home! He's hurt bad!"

For a moment, the sidewalk spun under my feet. Reeling from confusion and panic I cried again, "Not Benjy!" My feet took flight and I ran home like the wind, passing still more people along the way, all of them telling me to hurry home. I felt I was running a gauntlet, like in a movie where a young Native American brave had to run between fierce warriors who punched him as hard as they could to keep him from reaching the finish line.

When I got to our apartment building, a friend called out that Mom had gone to Hartford Hospital. It was on Seymour Street, several blocks away from where we lived, but I took no notice of the distance. I reached the hospital gasping for air just as a co-worker from the Royal Typewriter Company, where Mom worked, was helping her into his car. In a stupor, she looked right at me but didn't see me. The man told me to get inside and during the drive, I was able to piece the story together.

Benjy had not played with Brownie for long. He wanted to go outside to play, and a great-aunt, who was caring for him, let him go. There was nothing unusual about that. We typically played unsupervised in front of our tenement building or in the alley alongside. But this time, Benjy and his friends decided to visit an empty lot behind the Richard J. Kinsella School to play baseball.

One of the kids hit the ball onto the roof of a one-story building nearby, and Benjy climbed onto the roof to retrieve the ball. While there, several of the boys started throwing rocks at him. It was only meant as good-natured fun. They didn't mean to hurt him. But Benjy ducked the rocks and, stepping back, tripped over the edge of the roof and landed headfirst on the ground. In a panic, the boys left him at the scene. Someone eventually called the police, and Benjy was taken to the hospital.

Evening had now become night, and neighbors continued to gather at Tia Aurora's apartment for news from the hospital. Outside our small apartment, somber faces filled the wide hallway. Inside, Mom's disconsolate cries broke my heart.

Having never gone through anything like that before, I had a hard time dealing with the situation. What was happening to Benjy? I didn't want to talk to anyone. I sat alone in the room I had shared with my little brother and stared at the things that made up our life together. While the apartment had been cramped, it was still our little home.

I glanced at the plastic dog on the dresser and felt panic creeping into my heart with the image of Benjy playing in the room earlier that day. Guilt overcame me. If I had taken him with me, none of this would have happened. The clothes I had ironed the day before hung neatly in the closet. Mom always had us follow a tight routine, so we would learn to be self-sufficient and stay too busy to get into trouble.

The downstairs buzzer interrupted my thoughts, and the crowd in the hallway grew still. A moment later, muted footsteps scraped up the staircase like sandpaper on wood. After a pause, the footsteps echoed along the vinyl-tiled hallway toward Tia Aurora's apartment.

I peeked outside but only saw the crowd gathered around Tia Aurora's door. Silence. And then a wailing from Tia Aurora's apartment unlike anything I had heard in all my life. A cold chill came over my body, and my stomach twisted itself into a knot. I wanted to crawl into a fetal position and cry out to God, "Why?" But no words would come out of my mouth.

Benjy, my little brother, my very best friend in the world, was dead.

Chapter 14

ARE WE SO DIFFERENT?

Benjy's death shocked everyone. My poor mother seemed she would lose her mind with grief and had to be sedated daily. When the sedatives wore off, she would run into the bathroom and try to swallow whatever pills she could find to end her life. She thought of nothing but suicide. My aunts were ever vigilant and always managed to intervene in time.

Mom would sometimes suddenly fall to the floor with epileptic-like seizures. We had to be careful that she didn't bite her tongue. Thankfully, there were experienced hands around who seemed to know what to do.

One of the remedies was *Agua de Florida*, a rubbing alcohol mixed with water that smelled of citrus flowers and cinnamon and was popular among Latinos for its supposed healing properties. It came in a distinctive slender, long-necked bottle partially wrapped in silver foil. When my mom had one of her seizures, someone always managed to dampen a cloth or handkerchief with some *Agua de Florida* and pat her forehead. This concoction seemed to help her regain her composure. The comforting love and attention she received helped perhaps more than anything else.

Mom told neighbors she believed she was responsible for Benjy's death and that God was punishing her for divorcing my father. No one agreed with her, but that only seemed to convince her further that it was true.

Mom didn't know that I, too, blamed myself for Benjy's death. The thought kept running through my mind, "If only I could turn back time and take him with me to the Boy Scout meeting, he would still be alive." How selfish I had been. I had wanted to be the center of attention that day. For a few moments I got what I wanted—at an unthinkable and bitter price.

With my father gone and my mother a single woman, I was *el hombre de la casa*, the man of the house. As such, it was my duty to see to the funeral arrangements and talk with the life insurance company. The John Hancock Insurance Company agent, a genuinely nice man, made sure the funds were readily available to cover the various expenses and explained to me what I needed to do next.

My first appointment was at the O'Brien Funeral Home down the street. From there, I went next door to St. Simon's and was directed to the rectory where the priests lived. My heart pounding like a drum, I climbed the steps of the white-pillared building with its massive door that seemed to stretch to heaven. I had been taught this was a holy place.

After what seemed like an eternity, the door swung open. A young priest appeared in the doorway wearing a black, short-sleeved shirt with a white collar reaching to just under his Adam's apple. His apparel surprised me. Had I expected him to be wearing his Sunday robes? At his inquisitive look I blurted out why I had come. My little brother had died, I explained, and the people at the funeral home told me I needed to ask my church to schedule a re-qui-em (I had trouble with that word) ... a requiem Mass.

The priest rubbed the blond stubble on his chin and eyed me up and down. He stared at my shoes. I shifted my feet uncomfortably, knowing my shoes looked the worse for wear.

"Is your family a tithing member of the congregation?" he asked.

"Tie ... tith ..." I couldn't pronounce the word, nor did I know what it meant.

"Do you bring your offerings to this church?"

"Oh, yes sir! My brother and I come every Sunday ..." I paused. "Well, my brother and I *used* to come every Sunday, and we always put our pennies in the basket, three pennies in the first basket and two in the second!"

The priest pinched the bridge of his nose and murmured for a few seconds with his eyes shut. He seemed to be in some sort of pain, as though he had a headache. I noticed his voice sounded different from the priest who had heard my confession a few days ago.

"If you're not tithing members here, then you need to go to Sacred Heart."

"Sacred Heart?"

"Sacred Heart Church on the north end of town. Talk to the priest there."

"But we go to church *here*," I said with just a hint of protest. "My mom and I live down the block at 280 Main."

The priest narrowed his eyes and gave me a hard look. "You need to go to Sacred Heart."

"Why?"

"Because your people go to Sacred Heart Church. Near Albany Avenue and Main Street." And with that, he shut the door on me.

I didn't know what to do. My mother had always been strong in her faith in God and the Church and had raised me and Benjy to be good Catholic boys. We had been baptized as infants

118

and received holy sacraments every Sunday. After school, we'd go to catechism classes managed by tough nuns who enforced their authority with heavy wooden rulers. What a shock to think I had been attending the wrong church! But the towering door, now shut firmly in my face, seemed to indicate it was true.

I had never been on a bus alone, but I boarded one at the street corner and went in search of Sacred Heart, where "my people" attended church. The kindhearted bus driver dropped me off nearby, explaining how to reach the church on foot. I rounded the corner and came across a small, historic church building.

To my surprise, a white-haired priest greeted me. He wasn't Spanish, but he knew how to speak the language. He told me his name was Father Cooney and asked where I was from.

"I live at 280 Main."

"I haven't seen you here before," he said.

"I haven't been here before."

"Well, that would account for me not seeing you around the neighborhood," said Father Cooney with a smile. "What can I do for you?"

I lowered my head and grew silent, my emotions still raw. With a tightened throat I said, "I need to make ... arrangements ... for the funeral service."

"Funeral service?"

"My brother's dead."

Father Cooney bent down to look me more directly in the eye. "I'm sorry to hear about your bother. But you should have your service at St. Simon's, my son. That's the church closest to where you live."

"That's what I thought, too," I said. "But the priest at St. Simon's sent me here."

"What on earth for?" asked Father Cooney, scratching his silvery hair.

"He told me this is where my people attend church."

"*Your* people?" asked Father Cooney, turning red in the face.

"Yes, Father. I think he had a bad headache because he kept rubbing his temples."

"You come with me," said Father Cooney, taking off toward the back of the church. He stormed into his small office and began turning the dial on the telephone while muttering under his breath, "We'll see if they won't give your brother a proper service!"

Someone answered on the other end of the line. Evidently, he got the same priest on the phone as the one who had spoken with me earlier at the rectory. Father Cooney went directly to the point. After reminding the other priest of his vows to God, he promised to complain in the strongest terms to Church leadership if an invitation was not extended immediately to hold Benjy's funeral service at Saint Simon's.

After a few more moments, the priest hung up the phone with a loud clatter and looked at me, his face not quite as red as before. He put his hand on my shoulder. "Everything will be all right now," he reassured me. "Go home and I'll say prayers for you and your family."

I hesitated. "Father Cooney, I don't want to hold the service for my brother at St. Simon's."

Father Cooney straightened up and sighed. "You need to do it there, son. You can't let them get away with this. In America, we stick up for our rights."

"Can't you be the priest for Benjy's service?" I asked.

Father Cooney bent back down and searched my face. "Listen to me, son. People often see the outside of a person and pass judgment. God looks on the heart and sees His children. Go back to St. Simon's and tell that priest your brother is having his funeral service there. If anyone gives you any trouble, come and get me."

For the first time in days, a smile creased my lips. I nodded and walked away quietly. I turned at the entrance of the church and looked back to see Father Cooney still standing by his office. He waved, and I went on my way.

It isn't easy being the man of the house, I thought as I caught a bus back down Main Street to the South End.

When the day for Benjy's mass came, people filled the pews at St. Simon's. You might have thought an important dignitary had died instead of a ten-year-old boy. The church was brightly lit. When I saw my little brother lying motionless in his humble casket, I nearly fainted. I had to be held up by a friend, who helped me to a seat.

Mom sat on the front pew surrounded by her sisters and their husbands. Dad was conspicuously absent. I heard someone say it was probably too much of a shock for him, and his nerves couldn't handle it. I couldn't accept that. How about my mom and what she was going through? I decided at once that if I should die young, no one need bother telling my father. If he had not attended the funeral of his favorite son, he certainly wouldn't bother to attend mine.

Mom, dressed in black, clung to a white handkerchief she kept squeezing like a sponge. It soon became soaking wet. Every so often, she would look over at the coffin, as if she hoped for a miracle and Benjy would rise from the dead like Lazarus in the Bible.

The words of the requiem mass took on a distant drone like the sound of bees. The priest who had not wanted to officiate at the funeral stood at the altar in his luxurious robes, praying for Benjy's soul.

In turn, I spoke to God in my own prayer. In my grief, instead of having reverence for God, I blamed Him for taking my little brother away. I also reproached His Church for the insensitivity of one of their priests, forgetting what Father Cooney had done to rectify the wrong. It was easier to fault the Church and God. It was easier to vent my anger than to forgive. My prayer took on the form of an oath. I promised myself never to step foot inside a church again nor would I seek God as I had done in the past.

Such was the impact of Benjy's sudden death and my first blatant experience with discrimination in America. Surely, I may have been discriminated by someone in the past, but the fact that it came from a man of the cloth made the experience more bitter.

As Mom wept uncontrollably and seemed to age overnight by Benjy's death, I wondered if she yearned for a time when life was simpler. Might I convince her to return to *Borinquen* where we could re-make our lives under the blue skies of the Enchanted Island? Then again, how would that be possible without Benjy? His death had broken our hearts. He lay motionless in a casket, his head wrapped in white gauze giving him the look of a young sultan reclining peacefully in sleep. All the blood had been washed away, and his face was angelic.

I began to cry and cry and cry. My little brother, my best friend in the world, was gone. Who would ever be able to take his place?

In the weeks and months following Benjy's death, emptiness filled my life. I'd daydream about playing tag and hide-and-seek with my little brother. If I happened to see someone in the schoolyard who reminded me of him, I'd look for a place to hide and cry until there were no more tears to shed. When all the crying was over, of course, nothing had changed. The unspeakable loneliness and loss remained.

In my heartbreak and confusion, I nurtured the most selfish thought of all. With Benjy gone, my mother might begin to show me the special affection she had showered on her baby boy. Maybe my father would turn his thoughts toward me again. But the noise and grind of the city reminded me that life stops for no one, even when your own world has come to a crashing halt.

PART TWO

Entering a New Phase

LIVING BETWEEN CULTURES

Chapter 15

STANDING UP TO INJUSTICE

Mom's health declined after Benjy's death. Eventually, she returned to work, but at times *los ataques de nervios* (nervous convulsions) would drop her to the floor without warning. I tried to make as little trouble for her as possible. I continued shining shoes and babysitting for the neighbors whenever I could. I'd give Mom most of the money I made, and she'd set it aside in an old black purse.

At those times, I sensed a certain respect from her. But the sadness in her large, hazel eyes was never too distant. She acknowledged we needed the extra money and exhorted me to finish high school, maybe even go to college. She may have had the feeling that my doing well would somehow, even if only in a small way, bring some measure of meaning to Benjy's premature death. I don't know for sure. We were never able to talk for long without the concerns and labors of the day crowding their way into her heart and mind, and I would find myself alone again.

When school started in the fall, I tried my best to focus and get good grades. It wasn't easy. I suffered from undiagnosed Attention Deficit Disorder (ADD), but nobody knew much about it back then or how to treat it.

Grief could not last forever, at least not on the surface. Mom's beauty had always caught men's attention, and she was soon approached by a second cousin, Daniel Sierra, who wanted to court her. Eventually, he won her over. I didn't think we needed another man in the house, and I wasn't happy with Daniel's visits. About ten years younger than Mom, he had a slender build, jet-black hair, and was always well dressed.

Admittedly, he was a hard worker. From my vantage point on the street corner where I sold newspapers before school, I could see him working inside the Metropole Restaurant a few blocks north of 280 Main Street. He seemed to be in perpetual motion, waiting on customers, picking up dishes, and cleaning off tables, or cooking the special meat sauce used to cover the restaurant's popular, crunchy-skinned hot dogs.

Once Daniel set his mind on being with Mom, there was no keeping him away. His visits to our humble home continued until the two of them married. Then we moved as a new family to a larger two-bedroom apartment in our same building.

As I grew older and Mom focused on Daniel, I spent more time away from home. I got involved in community service by translating for Spanish-speaking migrants. It was a good feeling being able to help them apply for a driver's license or register their children for school.

I became increasingly aware that there was a much bigger world beyond our little corner of Hartford, Connecticut. On June 12, 1963, a year to the day that Benjy died, a white supremacist shot civil rights leader Medgar Evers in front of Evers' home in Jackson, Mississippi. It was a portent of things to come.

Later that year, President Kennedy was assassinated, and Malcolm X spoke ominously of the chickens coming home to roost and of armed black struggle in America.

In 1964, when I was in the eighth grade, a Community Action Agency (CAA) opened a couple of blocks from our apartment building. I gladly volunteered my time as a translator at the agency, which had been funded with federal grants provided by President Lyndon Johnson's War on Poverty. The CAA provided employment services and referrals to other social service agencies helping the poor.

Neighborhood Legal Services worked closely with the CAA. One lawyer, **Sydney Schulman**, counseled me and others about legal issues affecting the community. Some years later, he became the mayor of nearby Bloomfield, Connecticut. At the time, yearnings to become an attorney or social worker intrigued me.

It was an inspiring time for urban, community-minded Latino youths like me. We learned firsthand from the struggles of our African-American friends and got a real-life education on our constitutional rights as Americans. We became increasingly vocal in our challenge to the status quo, and repercussions followed.

A few months before my fourteenth birthday, I went to a *fiesta de bautismo* (baptism party) at an apartment building near the corner of Park Street and Main, a block from home. While the adults talked and laughed in the kitchen, I danced a slow song with my hostess, a dark-haired girl my age from school. Without knocking on the door, or asking permission to enter, a white police officer stepped into the apartment and took the needle off the vinyl record.

"All right, everybody!" he shouted. "I want to see all the adults right now!"

Everyone in the kitchen emptied into the living room. The officer informed them that there had been a complaint about a lot of noise coming from the apartment. He then said the party was over and ordered everyone to go home or be arrested.

I attempted to translate for the tenants, most of whom were talking all at once, but the policeman cut me off.

"That's enough, kid! If you want to help just tell 'em to go home," he said.

"Excuse me, officer, but have you ever heard of the Constitution of the United States?" I asked.

The policeman took a step toward me. His hand clenching his baton. "The Constitution?" he repeated sarcastically. "What do you know about the Constitution?"

"You have no legal right to walk into this apartment the way you did without a search warrant or asking permission."

The policeman's face turned red. "Well, well, what have we here? A smart Puerto Rican!"

"And a U.S. citizen," I said. "Just like you."

The police officer grabbed me by the shoulder and, immediately, two or three of the adults grabbed him. A scuffle broke out, more policemen arrived, and there were several arrests made. I was one of them.

As I was being directed into the police wagon, I saw Mr. Henderson, a black police officer I knew. He attempted to intervene on my behalf, explaining I was a good kid who was active in helping the community. He couldn't believe the charges that I had assaulted a policeman and resisted arrest. But his plea was ignored, and I was whisked away to the police station. In an ironic twist, one of the men taken to the city jail with me that night later saved an officer's life when the officer was attacked by a *machete*-wielding woman. This same woman had made the original complaint about the party.

Mom wasn't too happy to receive a late-night phone call telling her that her teenage son had been arrested and needed to be bailed out of jail. When she came for me, she didn't want to hear a word I had to say. She had an all-encompassing respect for the law. and her thinking was simple: if I had been arrested, I had done something wrong.

To my great surprise, my trial brought together several community leaders as character witnesses, including the president of the local chapter of the NAACP. I was grateful and humbled that an organization known for being a leader in the civil rights movement would reach out to help a young Puerto Rican from the South End.

My attorney obtained a mistrial based on the behavior of the judge who was blatantly prejudiced on the side of the police officer. With the case dismissed, the experience became a revelation for me about the inner workings of the judicial system and how powerful the support of a community can be when people unite behind a just cause.

After hearing the testimony of the various witnesses, Mom recognized the injustice that had been done and wasn't as upset with me as she had been at first. However, she continued to remind me from time to time that I could have saved myself a lot of trouble if I had not been out late at night—and if I had kept my mouth shut when confronted by the police.

I could agree with the late-night advice, but keeping my mouth shut when I saw an injustice being done was like telling a preacher to stop preaching. It went against everything I believed in and had been taught to hold dear. I was an American citizen and had rights guaranteed by the Constitution of the United States. I determined to be like the mentors who had extended themselves so unselfishly to me.

It followed, I suppose, that I would want to further identify with the poor in their work, literally, in the field of their labors.

LIVING BETWEEN CULTURES

Chapter 16

FIELDS OF SWEAT

Connecticut had a long history of producing some of the nation's finest tobacco. It was a tradition for young people to work the fields during summer vacations. My stepfather, Daniel, had worked the tobacco fields and saw no benefit in my working in them during the summer of 1964. I disagreed. To my idealistic way of thinking, there was something noble and pure about working the land, and it allowed me to show solidarity with the *campesinos*, the poor workers newly arrived from Puerto Rico and other Latin American countries.

Perhaps I also wanted to identify more closely with my father, who had gotten his start in America as a migrant farm worker. The work had been hard, but he had not backed away from it and had eventually brought us to the mainland to pursue the American Dream. From such humble beginnings, Puerto Ricans like my father had eventually migrated with their families all over the United States, including Hawaii and Alaska.

Things got off to a great start the first day of work. I boarded a yellow school bus with others my age, some of them friends, and we were driven just outside the city to a sprawling tobacco farm. We dragged our bottoms up and down the seemingly endless rows of tobacco plants as quickly as we could, removing the little buds (suckers) that grew at the bottom of the stalks. I was on my way to becoming a real man. The work was hard, but I did my best to stay focused on the reward, which also included a paycheck at the end of the week.

Later that evening, while I sat in front of the TV watching the CBS Evening News with Walter Cronkite, Mom came into the room to ask me how the day had gone.

"It went okay," I replied, shrugging in a confident sort of way.

"Do you have blisters?" Mom asked. "Show me your hands."

I grew defensive and kept my hands to myself. "Nuthin' to write home about."

"Write home? You live at home, *nene*."

"Don't worry, Mom. Like I said, everything's fine."

Mom spoke better English now, but she still had a hard time with slang expressions. She sat next to me and studied my face carefully, the way moms will do. Then she came to a conclusion.

"Don't let that sun make you *loco*," she said emphatically, tapping the side of her head and disappearing into the kitchen.

The next day was more of the same, but the soreness in my body made the work harder to manage. I had been expecting this adverse physical reaction initially but knew the solution was to work through the pain. My motto was, "If it doesn't kill you, it'll make you stronger."

By the fourth day, however, the anticipation of earning my first paycheck vanished. Every part of my body hurt, especially my seat. Even the pillow I wrapped around my bottom didn't help. A record high temperature added to the misery that day.

When I got home from work, Daniel intercepted me before I could drag myself into the shower. Drenched in sweat, I carried my uneaten lunch in its brown paper bag. When he learned some of the kids had nearly fainted in the terrible heat, he declared I would never work in the fields again. I didn't put up much of an argument.

I went into the bathroom and looked at my face in the mirror. My skin was burned, not bronzed. Every part of my body hurt, and my tongue felt as though it was stuck to the roof of my mouth.

That night, I was so exhausted, I couldn't sleep. I realized the agony my dad must have endured working for pitifully low wages in the farm fields of America. He had worked without complaint for months, not days, to send money home to Puerto Rico.

How did you do it, Dad? I wondered, my eyes finally growing heavy with sleep. *What force did you draw on? You must have been physically stronger than you looked.*

I turned slowly and painfully on my side and closed my eyes. Welcome sleep pulled me away like the sea tide off Santa Isabel. Further and further away I floated. The last thing I remember saying was *Gracias, Papá.* And then, somewhere between dreaming and being awake, I saw or imagined a figure with a bronzed face and strong, hard hands caked with dirt kneeling in a field of workers. He looked at me and smiled, a warm, friendly smile, the gracious smile of a *jíbaro.* He wanted to tell me something, but I fell asleep before he could speak.

Chapter 17

FEAR OF FAILURE

In case I had not drawn the appropriate conclusions from my brief experience as a farm laborer, Mom served me daily reminders of the need to focus on graduating from high school and perhaps attending college. No one in our immediate family had accomplished that goal and rarely talked about it.

Unfortunately, higher learning didn't seem to be in my future. I wasn't even sure I'd graduate as scheduled from Hartford High. I struggled terribly with the main courses needed to earn a diploma. My grades were best in subjects that caught my interest or were made exciting by the teacher. Whatever wasn't of interest literally bored me to sleep.

I became a regular visitor to the principal's office for lack of focus, talking, or fidgeting. I didn't intend to misbehave, and I believe my principal, Dr. Yeatman, realized I wasn't one of the "bad boys." As Mom had taught me, I showed respect for my teachers and was eager to please.

Dr. Yeatman must have known I was struggling with a learning problem and needed help. Teachers and other school personnel couldn't seem to pinpoint the reason I demonstrated a higher-than-average level of intelligence in tasks that demanded leadership, working with a diversity of students, and speaking, yet failed miserably in key academic courses and tasks that demanded my full attention. I couldn't understand how another student sitting beside me in class could read an assignment once and understand what was written, while I had to read it a half-dozen times to make sense of the material.

Clearly, my strengths lay in encouraging and helping others. I became a rare student leader that wasn't a member of the Honor Society. With the help of my favorite mentor, Miss Italia who taught English as a Second Language (ESL), I took the lead in starting an International Club for students of various ethnic backgrounds. Also, I became an inter-school exchange student, a member of the varsity wrestling team, and a community mediator in times of racial strife. But how could extracurricular activity help me succeed in life if I struggled so much with my schoolwork?

One day in the cafeteria, John, a neighborhood friend asked about my college plans.

"College?" I replied. "I'm not going to college, man."

"Why not?" asked John.

"Well, for one, I don't know what it's like or how to apply, and for another I don't think I'd be accepted if I did apply. If by some miracle a college took me in, I have no idea how I'd ever pay to go. I heard it's expensive."

John ignored my protests. "You can do it, Lou." he said. "Set your mind on it and you'll succeed. You have what it takes!"

I shook my head and prepared to leave. John held me by the arm.

"Look at your mom," he said.

"My mom?"

"She owns a business, right?"

I nodded. After Mom and Daniel married, they opened their own Puerto Rican restaurant called *Aquí Me Quedo* ("I'll Stay Here"), which in a relatively short time became well known throughout Connecticut for its outstanding food and service. People drove from as far away as Boston, nearly a hundred miles, just to sample Mom's cooking. The recipes were from her memory, and she was a fanatic about literally picking through every grain of rice and beans to perfect her specialty dishes.

"Didn't your mom go to college?"

"Mom never attended grade school," I replied.

John was taken aback. "You're kidding me."

"Why would I kid you? She grew up helping to take care of eight brothers and sisters and had me when she was twenty years old."

"Wow, I never knew that," he marveled. "And she's so beautiful!"

I scowled as John gathered his thoughts.

"Don't you see, Lou?" he continued. "Your mom has accomplished all that she's done *without* going to college or even high school. Imagine what you could do and how much you could help her if you had a college degree!"

I stared at John. I felt no anger toward him; if anything, I appreciated his concern. But he and I came from different worlds. His family considered higher education a minimum requirement, not a dream. How could he begin to understand the poverty and lack of scholarly self-esteem that dragged many down in my inner-city world?

Yes, I had ambition and had worked hard since I was a youngster. I understood that going to college was part of the American Dream, but it was hard to see how I could share in it. I was from a long line of farm laborers, now feisty migrants, in pursuit of even a small piece of the American pie. Heck, a few crumbs would do! And, when speaking of personal finances, anyone that has been in the restaurant business knows it takes years to become established. You can be doing fine today and be out of business in six months.

One thing about John—he was insistent. I wondered if my mother had secretly talked to him into pressuring me to get better grades.

"Okay, okay," I said finally. "I'll go to the guidance counselor and see what he says."

John smiled and went on his way. I felt as if he had pinned me to a mental wrestling mat.

A week later, I met with Mr. Gatlin, the guidance counselor, a rough-faced man who looked as though he'd rather have been somewhere else, perhaps on vacation in Cape Cod. He indicated for me to take a seat while he shuffled through my school records. In short order, he looked up and asked, "Why do you want to go to college?"

The negative tone of his voice disturbed me. "Well ... I ... I want to improve myself. I want to do better. I want to help my family and community."

Mr. Gatlin shook his head. "You don't have what it takes to get into college. You should consider becoming a mechanic, maybe a truck driver." Then he added, "Those are good jobs in case you didn't know."

I raised my voice in sudden annoyance. "Yes, I know they're good jobs, but I want to go to college!" I wasn't trying to be disrespectful, but my emotions took over.

Mr. Gatlin leaned forward in his chair as if to slap me. "Don't raise your voice at me, young man!" he shouted. "Who do you think you are?"

Abruptly, the meeting was over.

Later that night, I tried to sort out my conflicting thoughts and actions. Mr. Gatlin misinterpreted my raised voice as anger. Many Anglos didn't understand that talking passionately and at full volume was normal for many Puerto Ricans, whatever the subject.

As far as manual labor was concerned, almost all my family made a living working with their minds and hands, and I had a great admiration for their talents. My stepfather's uncle could handcraft a beautiful, small violin-shaped *"Cuatro"* guitar out of the wood of a discarded orange crate. Aunt Virginia's husband, Luis Romero, who we affectionately referred to as Tío Guiso, had little formal education or training, but was a genius for earning a living repairing broken electronic or mechanical items.

I spent many evenings with *Tío* who taught me how to assemble various working gadgets from pieces spread on his kitchen table. As much as I enjoyed taking things apart and putting them together again and loved how Tío

Guiso would use the gadgets to play pranks on the unsuspecting, I knew working with my hands wasn't my calling in life.

Perhaps Mr. Gatlin analyzed the situation further. Not long after our first meeting and after I joined another vocal minority student in complaining to school administration, the counselor called me to his office and agreed to place me in college preparatory classes.

I quickly began to think I had been set up for failure. Shakespearean English was foreign to me, and the language of advanced mathematics was worst of all. I enjoyed learning about the love between Romeo and Juliet but had little patience for English literature and subjects I believed I couldn't apply in real-life situations. As weeks became months, it appeared increasingly certain I would never be a student in an institution of higher learning. What I didn't know was that other people had more faith in me than I had in myself.

One glorious day, Dr. Yeatman introduced me to Mrs. Nesbitt, a soft-spoken, middle-aged African-American lady from Wethersfield, a nearby suburb of Hartford. She was exactly what I needed to break away from the fears that had bound me to my circumstances. We quickly became friends, and she patiently went to work trying to understand some of the learning challenges I faced.

Assisted by the constant nurturing of this sweet lady, my focus and self-esteem began to rise, as did my grades, and I applied to several colleges. My parents were grateful for Mrs. Nesbitt's educational outreach to their son. They had known I had the potential, but they had been unable to provide the academic guidance I needed due to their limited education.

A small but growing liberal arts college in Willimantic, Connecticut, responded to my letters. They contacted my high school and mentioned they had established a special program for applicants who might prove themselves in college if given the opportunity. One of their deans, Betty Tipton, a slender, red-headed lady with a heavy Southern accent, met with Mrs. Nesbitt and offered to interview me.

The moment I heard Mrs. Betty Tipton speak, I realized she was the exact opposite of the negative stereotype I had seen on television of southern white people. She was concerned about helping the disadvantaged, no matter their color.

"What do you feel will be your greatest struggle in college?" she asked.

Since I had heard about the parties held on some college campuses and being an impulsive young man, I answered, "The girls! Keep me away from the girls and I'll do just fine."

After a good laugh, she told me she would be willing to make a commitment to help me graduate from college if I would commit to the same goal. I gave her my word.

Not long after, I graduated from Hartford High and started my summer with a demanding schedule of remedial college course work. Mrs. Tipton took the helm, guiding me and several others through the rigors of college studies. There were certainly times when I felt I was in over my head and that I might not make it. But I dreaded the thought of letting my mother and the community down. Admittedly, I was also determined not to give Mr. Gatlin the satisfaction of saying "I told you so!" Fortunately for me, I was not alone. Mrs. Tipton kept her word and was unflagging in her commitment to my success.

Going home for a visit one weekend during my freshman year, I stopped at Mom's restaurant and ordered a Puerto Rican burrito, a special dish Mom created in honor of our Mexican friends. As I waited for the food to arrive, I looked around the restaurant Mom and Daniel had worked so hard to build into a successful business. A framed letter from the Governor of Puerto Rico hung on the wall, as well as pictures of Mom with celebrities and local political figures. One photo of Mom with a local beauty queen who had participated in the state Puerto Rican parade festivities especially caught my eye.

I turned to find Mom standing next to the table with my food.

"I told the beauty queen you're a nice boy," she said with a knowing smile.

I groaned. "You did what?"

"And you need a nice girl."

"Mom," I protested. "What're you doing? That's embarrassing."

"It's true, isn't it? You need a nice girl."

"I've met a lot of nice girls."

"Just don't let them get in the way of your studies, *mijo*. We don't want anything to interfere with your education."

"No, Ma, of course not."

"*Estoy orgullosa de ti,*" ("I'm proud of you") she said, setting down the Puerto Rican burrito and giving me a kiss on the forehead.

I breathed in the delicious aromas and glanced at Mom. She was smiling happily, and I thought of telling her about the girl I had met just a week ago. Then I took a taste of the food, and all I could think about was wiping the plate clean. Mom nodded with satisfaction and returned to the kitchen.

Chapter 18

IMPULSIVITY OF YOUTH

The day started off innocently. Always eager to serve, I responded to a call for volunteers at a community dance held in my college town of Willimantic. That's where I saw her moving across the dance floor to the rhythmic *salsa* music of Willie Colón and Héctor Lavoe. *Salsa* music and dancing had long been a passion of mine, and I was drawn to Adriana like a bee to pollen.

The evening held an easygoing atmosphere, and I took a few turns with her between my volunteer duties. We could have won a dance contest that night. Everybody had a great time, and when the *fiesta* ended sometime near midnight, I was in great spirits.

After a night of good, clean fun, I knew I needed to head home and get some sleep. I had an important class assignment to finish the following day.

But I volunteered again, this time to give people a ride home. Adriana, among others, piled into my car. A gradual tightening in my chest increased as I dropped people off one by one until only Adriana remained. When she asked me to show her where I lived, I obliged. With my roommates out for the evening, I had the place to myself. A stronger individual might have shaken his head clear in that moment and taken Adriana home immediately.

I was new to the independence offered by college life and inexperienced in how to respond in moments like this. I didn't know that much about intimate relations; my parents had never talked to me about the birds and the bees. I would find those things out on my own.

Parked in front of my apartment building, I turned to Adriana, her face softly lit in the shadows. Without thinking, we leaned over and kissed. One thing led to another, and we spent several hours in my room.

Two months later, I went home for the weekend and helped out in the kitchen at Mom's restaurant.

"*Luis! Telefono!*" Daniel shouted.

"Who is it?" I asked.

Daniel shrugged. He didn't know, and he was too busy to ask. I set down the mop, wondering who'd be calling so late at night. People called to order food or speak with a family member, but the restaurant was closed for the evening.

"Hello?"

"Luis, this is Adriana."

"Adriana?"

"From Willimantic."

Images of the night we spent together flooded my mind. I leaned against the wall, held the telephone a little closer, and projected a softer tone.

"Hi ... how you doin'?"

"I'm pregnant."

"Excuse me?"

"I'm pregnant."

I looked down at the floor and turned my back toward my parents, speaking quietly.

"Can you repeat that?"

"I'm pregnant."

"I don't understand."

"I'm going to have your baby."

When I heard "baby," I froze. My throat tightened and I couldn't speak. This was a life-changing event I wasn't prepared for, and I was overwhelmed with fear and concern about my family's future and Adriana's.

How could this be happening? Our situation wasn't anything new in the neighborhoods we lived in. The irony was, when other neighborhood friends found themselves in the same predicament, I would be among those judging them for their reckless actions. Now it was my turn.

After a few moments, Mom approached, her forehead creased in concern. My body language must have tipped her off.

"What is it, *mijo*?"

Still struggling to make sense of the news, I covered the mouthpiece of the telephone.

"Someone's ... pregnant."

Mom stared at me, her mouth open. She raised her eyebrows.

"I met a girl in Willimantic ..."

"What do you mean?"

"I mean, I met a girl in Willimantic."

"And she got pregnant?"

"We were dancing."

Mom continued to stare at me. "And she got pregnant?"

"Who're you talking to?" Adriana asked.

"I'm talking to my mom."

"You're telling her?" Adriana raised her voice in unbelief, embarrassed that I would be sharing this news without discussing it with her first.

"I tell my mom everything."

Daniel, now aware something upsetting had happened, joined Mom in peppering me with questions. How old was she? Who were her parents? How long had I known her? How did she know I was the father? They wanted me to have a conversation with them and relay their questions to Adriana simultaneously, which I did as best I could.

Then came the big question.

Mom leaned in close, stared intently into my eyes, and asked, "Do you want to marry this girl?"

Instinctively, I put my hand over the telephone mouthpiece as if I was going to say something. But no words came out. I bit my lip instead. I did not want to marry anyone. I was too young to get married. I wanted to finish college. However, none of that negated the fact I had impregnated a girl.

"I have the idea!" Mom shouted. Daniel and I both turned to look at her. "Tell her we raise the baby! You don't get married. Finish college like you say. But the baby comes and lives with us."

I relayed my mother's proposal to Adriana, but she didn't care much for the idea. After several minutes of talking back and forth, Adriana reached her decision.

In a tone of disappointment, she said, "If you don't want to marry me, then I'll raise the baby myself."

I hesitated. I knew what she wanted to be done, but how could I do it? We hardly knew each other and, most importantly, we hadn't had time to fall in love. My mind was overwhelmed with unanswered questions. What would Adriana say when she was asked who the child's father was or where he was? Would I ever meet the child? Would he or she forgive me for not being a part of his or her life? And the inevitable question: would I ever be sure the baby was mine?

What I resented most about my own father and many fathers in general was how little time they invested in the lives of their children. This time, there was the chance I would become the absentee dad. Adriana's voice broke into my thoughts a final time.

"I won't bother you anymore."

After a click, the telephone line fell silent.

I changed that night. Who wouldn't? Daniel offered me a piece of pie, but I had no appetite and insisted on going back to the apartment alone. I felt terrible about all those I was disappointing, especially the innocent child being brought into the world without a father present. But I also felt Adriana had acted more courageously for assuming the responsibility of raising the child without me. She had demonstrated her strong will and independence.

Yet a feeling of relief rose inside me. I was in full pursuit of the American Dream, and one phone call had threatened to derail my plans.

"The crisis is over for now, and someday I will meet this child." I repeated the words to myself over and over.

I took in deep, calming breaths as I walked. But in my innermost being I knew this would not be the last crisis I would encounter. I couldn't bring myself to contemplate where this encounter with life's challenges would lead.

Chapter 19

THE RIOTS

I received a letter several months later instructing me to report for the draft. It was February 1969 and with the Vietnam Conflict at its height, every eligible American male over eighteen was called up for military service. But why was *I* being called? I was a full-time college student and had an exemption. Clearly, it must be a clerical error, but I decided I should report to keep myself out of trouble. The Army representative at the New Haven induction center agreed that it was likely a mistake but advised me to complete the process before bringing the error to the college's attention.

As I stood in line with other draftees and recruits waiting for our physical exams, several guys in front of me discussed their plans to avoid the draft. Many young men unhappy with the Vietnam Conflict had attempted to beat the system. Some moved to Canada and others devised their own methods. They gave all kinds of reasons for exemption, from having flat feet to being homosexual, as if the confessions would trick the doctors and save them from being drafted. After the doctor asked the required questions, almost everyone was told, "You're fine. Next!"

I had to smile. The whole thing became more and more surreal as I endured the poking and prodding. I had no quarrels with the US military. Many Latinos had successful careers in service to our country. In fact, Puerto Ricans had received many awards for their service, including the Medal of Honor. However, what provoked the protests of many of the flower children and others of my generation was Washington, DC's insistence on extending this most unpopular war and not seeming to care about the daily reports of young men killed.

After the medical examinations were completed, a group of us were told to take our seats inside a classroom and fill out various forms. A staff sergeant walked among us telling us what to do and adding that we had the right to appeal to his commanding officer if he couldn't answer a question to our satisfaction.

I was doing fine until I had to check a box indicating my race. Hmmm ... There were only three choices. I didn't consider myself Caucasian, and I wasn't Negro, and I wasn't Oriental. So, I raised my hand.

"Yes, sir," said the sergeant, recognizing me.

"Yes sir, Mr. Sergeant," I said. "I don't know how to answer this question."

"Which question is that?"

"The one about my race. I don't know what to put down."

"You don't know your race, son?"

"I don't think you understand."

"What don't I understand?" said the sergeant, laughing. "That's an easy question."

"It's not easy for me, sir."

"Just put down white. That ain't complicated."

"But I'm a Puerto Rican. I'm a mixture of a lot of different people. I got African blood, I got native Taino Indian blood, and I got European blood. Who knows, I probably have a little Asian blood in me, too."

"Well, never mind all that. You look white enough to me. Just check off white."

I started to check off the box next to the word "white" but stopped myself. I didn't want to be forced into the accepted practice in the states of classifying people by color or race.

"Sir," I shot back.

"What now?"

"You said that if we had a question that you couldn't answer to our satisfaction, we had the right to appeal to your commanding officer."

"I did say that, didn't I?"

"Yes sir, you did."

"What's your name, soldier?"

"Rivera, sir. Luis Rivera." I was about to add, *and I'm not a soldier yet,* but I remembered Mom's warnings about keeping my mouth shut.

"And you think you need to talk to the C.O."

"If that isn't too much trouble?"

The sergeant stared at me in silence. "I'll be right back, Rivera," he said finally.

A couple of minutes later, a young-looking officer came into the room. "Who is Louis Rivera?" he asked.

I raised my hand. "I am."

"Sarge tells me you have a problem with one of the questions," said the officer.

"Yes, sir. It's this question here about race. As I told the sergeant, I'm a Puerto Rican. I have African blood in me and Taino Indian blood and European blood. And there's no box I can check off for who I am. What do I do?"

"Well, if you had to pick a race to identify yourself, which one would it be?"

I looked back at the form and tapped my pencil a few times on the desktop. "Well, sir, if you really want to know, I guess I'd have to say I'm a member of the human race."

The classroom erupted into hoots and hollers as the recruits voiced their approval. The officer turned red in the face.

Once the clamor had died down a little, the officer said, "Very well, then. If that makes you happy, write that down."

"Write it down where?"

"Just write it in the margin." And then he left the room.

The following week, I went to the school's registrar and sorted out the problem. Sure enough, it had been a clerical error. I should not have been ordered to report to the induction center.

The evening television news broadcasted images of the devastation and carnage brought about by the war. Some of my high school alums served in Vietnam and returned in caskets. While willing to fight to defend myself and my country, I wasn't in a hurry to volunteer quite yet. Other conflicts closer to home needed my attention.

The race riots that shook America in the late Sixties and early Seventies didn't spare Hartford, and I found myself in the thick of things. During the hot summer nights when I was home from school and police wearing riot gear patrolled our streets, I joined other passionate voices of the Spanish community in the South Green area trying to bring peace to my neighborhood streets.

Numerous times I had to be escorted through the South Green area by members of the clergy to escape the angry clutches of bikers or misinformed *gringos* who saw me and our community as a threat to their way of life.

The city administration established a citizens' committee to foster peace and invited me to be a member. Still, more often than we wanted, violence erupted as Hartford's North and South Ends grew increasingly on edge with rioting, shootings, and accusations of police misconduct.

I regularly left the safety of my small college campus of Willimantic to help mediate. Names like Mao Tse-tung, Karl Marx, Vladimir Lenin, and Che Guevara crept into the conversations of young people, as the horror stories and frustrations from the riots continued to mount up and militant groups like the Black Panthers and Young Lords gained popularity.

One summer night, the conflict became directly personal. With seemingly no provocation, police cordoned off the street in front of our building and tossed teargas canisters near the entrance. Panic ensued when the gas wafted into some of the apartments, causing the tenants to choke and feel as if ground glass was being rubbed in their eyes. I watched in anger as desperate mothers held their infant children near open windows or tried leaving the building for scarce fresh air.

When the police ordered them to return to their apartments, I screamed in Spanish for the tenants to evacuate and join me as I sat on the sidewalk curb in a non-violent gesture. Out of frustration one policeman pointed his shotgun barrel at my head and ordered me to go back inside the building. Within seconds, though it seemed like an eternity, a police sergeant ordered the officer to lower his weapon and allow the tenants to peacefully sit on the curb. Heaven only knows the lives that were spared that night by the intervention of that sergeant. Sadly, I was too enraged at the entire incident to thank him for his intervention.

Earlier that same night, a Puerto Rican policeman with a good reputation in our neighborhood was relieved of duty because he refused to carry out the orders of a superior officer. He had been ordered to arrest a group of people gathered on the street that he believed had not broken any laws. The Latino community was disappointed, but not surprised, when we learned he had resigned from the force. Tragically, he was one of the voices of reason we had in the police ranks, as well as one of the few Latino cops on the beat.

On another night, after trying to reason face to face with the Mayor of Hartford about what the community felt were the strong-arm tactics of some of the local police officers, an older black man approached me and abruptly began to preach.

"Son, what do you think this rioting and protesting is accomplishing? Don't you know that the greatest revolutionary who ever lived was a man of peace? He never hurt anyone. People have come and gone, but his name lives on."

There was something about this man's passionate proclamation that irritated me. "Really?" I asked. "Who was that?"

The older man looked at me with such a kind, loving expression I began to feel ashamed. He said in almost a whisper, "Don't you know, son?"

"I said I don't know, mister. Who is he?"

"His name is Jesus Christ."

I was speechless. I couldn't believe that in the middle of all the turmoil around me, some misguided stranger was talking to me about Jesus. My frustration grew.

"You know what, sir?" I said. "As far as I'm concerned, this isn't the time or the place to be talking about spiritual matters. Why don't you just move on and stay off the streets. You can get hurt out here! This is the real world where real people are dealing with real-life issues. I think you need to take your beliefs home with you and leave the struggle to the people!"

No one seemed to disagree with me, and I turned back to the old man. His expression surprised me. I had been less than cordial in front of a group of people, and he gazed upon me with large, tearful eyes filled with kindness and deep concern. My first instinct was to turn away, but my pride was too strong. Slowly, the old man continued down the street, merging eventually into the crowd and disappearing in the dark.

Everyone promptly forgot about him, but I would never forget the words he spoke that night. In later years, I would wonder if he might have been an angel sent to show me that the love of one man has meant more to the world than the rioting and wars of many. A quest to understand the depth of the minister's words would not happen until I had exhausted every possibility to first make peace with the world on my own terms.

Chapter 20

NUYORICAN GIRLS

In the fall of 1970, the war in Vietnam showed telltale signs of winding down. Young men were still being drafted and Vietnam remained a killing field, but I tried to focus on my studies and stay out of trouble, as I entered my third year at Eastern Connecticut State. Any young person can attest, however, that love can create all sorts of unexpected mischief and changes in one's life.

Her name was Norma Acevedo, and she was seventeen years old when love's arrow pierced my heart. I was infatuated with Norma from the moment I saw her. With her olive complexion, jet-black hair, and tall slender figure, she looked as if she had walked out of a fashion magazine. Little did I know she had been voted the "Best Dressed Girl" in her high school.

When I learned she was from New York, I was even more determined to win her over. Ever since I had lived in the Bronx, I had always had an interest in the pretty *señoritas* from the Big Apple. They were beautiful, sophisticated, and they dressed so fashionably! The only drawback was that some of the girls sprinkled their speech with profanity and probably didn't even realize it. But I could work with that!

I made Norma the target of my affections. What attracted me most about her, and continues to this day, was the way she carried herself. She was not only taller than the average Latina, she had a classy air that projected confidence without being pretentious. I felt she was the perfect partner for me.

We met on a rainy day at a *fiesta* at Wesleyan University in Middletown, Connecticut, where a group of Hispanic college students had gathered to discuss strategies for increasing college recruitment among minorities. I'm afraid I didn't make much of an impression when I walked through the door wearing a drenched, olive-green rubber poncho.

When I saw Norma, I turned to my friend, Andy, and said, "You see that tall girl over there? She's going to be my wife!"

Andy chuckled in disbelief. He knew about my fervent refusal to marry until I finished my education and was at least in my forties. This time was different, and I knew it. Standing before me was my soulmate and future mother of our children. The more I gazed upon her, the more I could picture us as a happily married couple, aging gracefully together. However, I didn't tell her that.

Norma hardly gave me a glance when I first approached her. However, she noticed the nicely fitted suit beneath my poncho, which made a better impression. She still ignored me.

After introducing myself, her answer to my continuous query about a date was, "First of all, I already have a boyfriend. Second, I'm not interested, and third, you're not my type."

I put both hands over my chest and winced. "But does your boyfriend love you?"

"Of course, he loves me."

I had always felt confident about my gift of speech, and it wasn't long before I began prying information from the tall beauty. She was nearing her eighteenth birthday and in her first year at the University of Connecticut (UCONN), which was minutes away from my school.

Since I wasn't getting anywhere with my diplomatic approach, my upper-classmen's ego took over, and I impulsively blurted out a prediction.

"If you don't want to go on a date with me, remember this: When you turn eighteen, you will be mine!"

I had been told I had a nice smile, and I turned it on for Norma at full power. Her response was lightning fast. She gave me a stare that could have cut me in half and let out a few choice New York City expletives that made me blush. Then she gave me the cold shoulder.

Not one to give up easily, I kept trying to gain her attention, as the weeks and days to Norma's eighteenth birthday approached. Out of desperation, I asked her best friends at the university, Brunie and Anna, what they could share with me about Norma's likes and dislikes.

"I'm in love with her!" I said. "Can't she see that? Feel my head, I think I have a fever."

The girls laughed, and Anna said, "Louie, you can be so crazy."

"But don't you think we're meant for each other?" I persisted. "We make the perfect couple, don't you agree?" I stood and walked around the dorm foyer with my right arm bent at the elbow, as though I were leading Norma to the ball.

"I think you're a nice guy. I told Norma so." Anna added.

"And what'd she say?"

Brunie looked puzzled.

"Well?" I said. "Come on. You can tell me."

"Gimme a break, Louie, I'm tryin' to remember. Norma said you move a little slower than the boys in the city. And she doesn't feel right dating you even though she and her guy aren't as close as they once were."

Another punch to the gut.

"Just because I don't live in the Bronx anymore doesn't mean I'm a hick! I can pick up my pace, and it's good to know that I may have a chance, especially if she and her boyfriend may be breaking up." I gave the girls a hard look. "I can change," I said with an air of mystery.

The girls stared at me, and then Brunie looked at her watch. "We gotta get goin', Louie."

"Tell me something," I said, reaching out to stop them from leaving. "Why does Norma want to be a vet? A pretty girl like that getting animal hair and slobber all over her hands and clothes. It doesn't seem to suit her at all if you ask me."

Brunie stared at me. "You really are country, aren't you?"

"What do you mean?" I asked, unable to keep a defensive tone from my voice.

"Norma loves animals," said Brunie.

"*Loves* animals?"

"Yeah, of course!" she said, standing to leave for real. "She's motivated by love."

"Wait!" I said. "What kind of animals?"

"All kinds," Anna said.

I jumped to my feet. "You mean, like a parrot?"

They both made faces.

"A cat? All girls like cats, right?"

Brunie shook her head. I don't know what she saw in me at that moment, but I guess she must have felt sorry for me because she proceeded to let me in on a little secret that turned out to be a key to Norma's affections.

A couple of weeks later, in November, Norma turned eighteen. In league with her friends, as well as mine, I planned a surprise birthday party, picking up Norma and some of her *amigas* at their UCONN dormitory and taking them for a ride. To keep Norma from guessing what we had planned, I intentionally started an argument with her. I then told her Andy wanted us to stop by before continuing.

When the door opened, all our friends shouted "Happy Birthday!" Norma was stunned. Then I showed her my gift. Inside a box with holes on the top and tied with a yellow ribbon, something moved and whined. Norma took off the bow, opened the box, and was immediately licked in the face by the cutest little black-and-brown Beagle-mix puppy you've ever seen.

"You really do love me!" she exclaimed, her eyes filling with tears.

The little secret given to me sealed the deal. On her eighteenth birthday, she was mine.

Less than a year later, in my senior year of college, I broke my childhood promise of not returning to a church and married Norma Acevedo in the Bronx. Because we were both still in school, we agreed to honeymoon later in Europe. We had no idea when that would be or how we would afford it. We were young and in love and, as everyone knows, love makes a way for dreamers.

LIVING BETWEEN CULTURES

Chapter 21

FAKING IT

Much of the fighting in Vietnam was nearing its end by the time I graduated from college in the summer of 1972. It was time to find employment in the real world. Law school would have to wait until I could afford it, probably longer since I couldn't see myself reading, writing and laboring over volumes of law books.

Norma and I moved to Hartford and rented an apartment with a small loan from a local bank co-signed by my Aunt Virginia and Uncle Guiso. We began searching for work opportunities. Norma found a position with Catholic Family Services in Hartford. Having volunteered with some of the social service agency programs, I knew the constant uncertainty agencies went through in finding funds to continue providing services. I needed steady employment. Working for an inner-city anti-poverty program didn't seem like the right choice for me.

Ironically, the public affairs representative for one such agency informed me about interviews being conducted for the position of a television news reporter at Channel 30, the local NBC affiliate in West Hartford. I had long been a fan of news anchorman Walter Cronkite and would sometimes stand in front of a mirror acting as if I was delivering the news. With Norma's encouragement, I took a chance and asked for an interview. She thought I had the presence of an anchorman.

Dressed in my Sunday best, I met Bob Douglas, the news director. The first question he asked was about my prior experience. I squirmed uncomfortably in my seat.

"I don't have any, well, unless you include the time I was interviewed by television and newspaper reporters during the riots."

"I see."

"Did I tell you I'm a college graduate?"

"What did you study?"

"Applied Social Sciences."

Mr. Douglas glanced at his watch. "Do you have any writing samples?" he asked.

"What kind of writing samples?"

"A news report. A term paper. Anything."

"I, uh ... I didn't bring any."

"How about an audition tape?"

"No, sir."

Mr. Douglas stared at me for several seconds without saying anything. "Tell me again why you're applying for this job?"

I cleared my throat. I didn't have a portfolio of writing samples or an audition tape to show him, but I had gone to the library earlier in the week and studied up on the business of television, its marketing and ratings. Going to college had taught me how to use a library well.

"Well, sir, I believe that when you put me in front of the camera and people in the Latino community hear my name on television, your ratings are going to increase."

"Is that so? What makes you think that?"

I could tell he was amused by my brash confidence. I leaned toward him across the table. "Do you know how many Latino people live in Connecticut, Mr. Douglas?"

"How many are there?"

"There are thousands of us!"

"That many."

"Yes, sir. And they all watch TV."

"That doesn't surprise me."

I took advantage of his increased interest to continue. "And are you aware, sir, that there is no television news program anywhere in our state even trying to reach the Latino audience? To me, it's logical. Put a newsperson in front of the camera who is Latino, who shares their culture, and the audience is sure to follow."

"You may have a point there. Do you have any recommendations?"

I sat up in my chair. "Absolutely! Me, of course."

Mr. Douglas chuckled. "You're just out of college with zero experience. It's easier said than done. Why should I hire you?"

"Put me in front of your cameras and see for yourself, sir!

He continued smiling. Then he called my bluff. He pushed the talk button on his desk intercom. "Have Leo come to my office," he said.

Leo was the affiliate's studio director. At Mr. Douglas's direction, he escorted me to a darkened news set and flipped on the brightest lights I had ever seen. Startled, I recognized the set used on the evening news. I flushed with exhilaration when told to sit in the anchorperson's chair.

"Do you have any copy to read?" Leo asked.

"No."

"Do you want to write any?

I considered this, then asked, "Do you have anything I can read from?"

Leo rifled through papers on a desk and handed me some old copy. He instructed me to watch for the red light on top of the television camera to turn on. For fifteen minutes I imagined being the renowned anchorman Walter Cronkite providing the evening news, though without his deep voice, and gave it my best.

My confidence won the day. Out of numerous applicants, Mr. Douglas offered me the position. He saw my potential and gave me an opportunity that I greatly appreciate to this day. He was willing to be open to new ideas and take the risk.

Over the next months, I learned the ins and outs of my new profession with the help of an African-American videographer, Moses Price. I could not have survived or developed in my craft without his mentoring. He was knowledgeable about the media and local politics.

The first lesson he taught me proved to be key: "Fake it till you make it!" he said.

Moses taught me how to hold a microphone, where and how to stand in front of the camera, and a lot more. He guided me patiently through the many potential pitfalls I confronted early on, and he helped me understand and appreciate my ethical responsibilities as a journalist.

I quickly learned that television is a powerful medium of communication and that a microphone and camera in the right hands can be a great equalizer when reporting an injustice or applying pressure on the powers that be to make needed changes in the community.

I also learned there is no such thing as a truly unbiased news report. Every incident can, and probably should be, reported from a variety of perspectives. People tend to view things through their own prisms. My challenge was to report on the news as objectively as I could, and I deliberately toned down my community involvement in order to remain free of the charge of bias.

But that didn't stop me from addressing the pressing social issues affecting my community, which led me to meet and interview César Chávez of the United Farm Workers Union. I produced a documentary on the plight of the migrant day laborers he was working diligently to help. I also produced and co-hosted a bilingual variety show once a week that received great support from the Latino community. The Puerto Rican community was especially supportive after native son and comedian Jose Miguel Agrelot, known as "Don Cholito," appeared on the show.

From the world's perspective of success, I was clearly on my way up the ladder. Six months into my job with Channel 30, Norma and I decided it was time to buy a house in the suburbs, the next step in our pursuit of the American Dream. We set our sights on nearby Newington and purchased a starter home, a small, detached, two-bedroom, with a large backyard and swimming pool.

Norma was somewhat apprehensive because we signed a long-term mortgage with a higher monthly payment than our apartment rental had been. At the time, no one in either of our immediate families had any experience owning a home stateside. But I was confident we'd make everything work. We were *Boricuas* after all, inventive, scrappy, and resilient!

We couldn't wait to invite family and friends over to see the house. Sadly, Mom and Daniel only came over once or twice. They claimed to be busy with the restaurant in Hartford.

I knew better. Mom believed that, after more than twenty years of hard work and faithful duty raising a family, she had accomplished her mission in the States. She was ready to go back to *Borinquen,* the land she considered home. I tried to convince her otherwise. Apart from loving her with all my heart, she was a strong, stabilizing influence in my life, and I would miss her. I had always benefited from her insights and wisdom.

After a year at Channel 30, Norma and I took our long-awaited honeymoon, backpacking through Europe for several weeks. We had a great time meeting people from different cultures and enjoying their cuisine. Not many months later, we discovered a baby was on the way. Everything was working out better than I could have imagined!

Mom, happy to hear that Norma was pregnant, shared her own news. She and Daniel had leased the restaurant and were leaving for Puerto Rico within the month. A few days later, I stopped at the restaurant to say goodbye.

I chose the slow part of the day to visit. When I went to *Aquí Me Quedo* during the busy lunch hour, usually accompanied by Moses Price who loved Mom's cooking, she liked to call me out in front of all the patrons to help her wash the dishes, pots, and pans. I would dutifully remove my Channel 30 navy-blue blazer, tuck my necktie into my button-down shirt, roll up my shirtsleeves, and go to work.

"Hey everybody!" Mom would shout with mischievous glee. "This is my TV reporter son, Luisito, washing dishes. He's not so big-shot after all!"

But today I came by in the quiet of late afternoon. Mom urged me to eat something, but I declined. I poured myself a cup of *tamarindo* juice, and we sat at a corner table.

"Why you look so sad?" Mom asked. "You act like we won't see each other again."

"I'm gonna miss you, Ma, and I don't want you to go. Are you sure you won't change your mind about leaving us?"

"I told you already. I don't belong here anymore, *mijo*."

182

"How can you say that? You have a grandbaby on the way."

"I don't want to interfere."

"We've already talked about all that. You won't be interfering."

"Mothers-in-law mean well, but they should leave couples to work things out. In the end, it could cause problems like I experienced with your father."

"This is different. Norma thinks the world of you." I paused. "I think the world of you."

Mom grew quiet.

"You and Dad had some problems," I continued.

"And you don't have any problems?" Mom replied testily.

"None of what happened with you and Dad is happening with me and Norma. We have a good life."

Mom again fell silent for a moment, then reached across the table and touched me on the cheek.

"I'll build you a separate room," I said.

"No thank you."

"Then how about a house down the street? I've seen some houses for sale."

"Daniel won't want that."

I looked to where Daniel was tidying up in the kitchen. I knew he'd agree if Mom were of a mind to stay.

"Anyway," continued Mom. "I'm tired of the cold, and I have your college diploma to take with me. My son got a college education and my job is done. Now I will return to my hometown."

I lowered my head. I didn't win many arguments with Mom, but she was wrong about this one.

"I really think you should reconsider. Your grandbaby will be raised without you near."

"You call me if there're problems."

Mom gazed at me. I turned away from her large hazel eyes. Disappointment and hurt overwhelmed me. I had been rejected, again.

"Don't forget who you are, *nene*."

"Who am I, Ma?"

"You're a *jibarito* (a country boy) from Santa Isabel. Don't ever forget where you came from."

My voice rose. "I'm also living in America, Ma! That makes me an American, too!"

Mom shrugged. "Then you're an American *jibaro*. But all this dreaming about a big, fancy life, being famous and all that ... be careful, son. Don't let it go to your *cabeza*."

Her eyes held me in a warning gaze. I threw my hands in the air. Daniel came out of the kitchen, and I shook his hand, hugged and kissed Mom on the cheek, and returned home to Norma in Newington.

When I drove by the restaurant two weeks later, new management had already taken over.

Moses wanted to check out the food, but I convinced him to have lunch at one of the Italian restaurants farther down on Franklin Avenue.

Our son, Luis Daniel, came into the world three months later in December. We named him after his two grandfathers, Luis Acevedo and Daniel Sierra, and called him Danny. He was a breakout hit. Our little chubby bundle of joy was born with a full head of dark hair and the longest black eyelashes. Talk about baby worship.

Norma's mom, Victoria, came from the Bronx with her other children. While the women helped decorate his new crib with fancy bows and a gold-colored quilt, Norma's two younger brothers kept busy washing and polishing our used Fiat sportscar.

It saddened me that Mom was not present to share in the joy and celebration. As I could attest from my own experience with Abuela Geña and Abuelo Filoquío in Puerto Rico, grandparents have a way of making a difference in the lives of grandchildren. But such thoughts were mostly in passing. My career was about to go into overdrive.

PART THREE

The Other Side

Chapter 22

REACHING FOR THE STARS

There he was on prime time—intrepid New York City reporter Geraldo Rivera, star of WABC-TV's news team. With cameras rolling, his break-down-the-door style produced results that were hugely popular with viewers. Did I look up to him and seek to emulate him? Of course, I did! He was six years my senior and had won a prestigious Peabody Award in 1972 for his exposé of the horrific abuse suffered by mentally disabled students at the state-run Willowbrook School in Staten Island. Not only that, he was a proud Puerto Rican on his father's side.

Imagine my excitement when I received a call in April 1975 from Adam Cousins, a corporate executive with a national broadcasting company I will call United States Television (UST) in New York City. Mr. Cousins was in the process of replicating the successful *Exclusive News* format at UST-owned-and-operated stations around the country. I had come onto his radar screen as a potential recruit. At the time of the call, I had been with WHNB for a little under three years.

As with all major decisions, I discussed the invitation with Norma, and we were both excited about the possibilities. I discreetly took a day off from work and made the trip to Manhattan to meet with this innovative executive. His office overlooked Madison Avenue.

Bursting with energy, friendly, and enthusiastic, Mr. Cousins was five years older than I and had been born and raised in New Jersey. I liked him immediately. He was determined to make news reporting at UST more upbeat and dynamic with reporters that reflected a younger demographic. I deduced that was a big part of the reason he had sought me out.

"That's great to know, Mr. Cousins, but I hope you understand I'm a rookie at this game and still have a long way to go as a reporter. You see, I never took any journalism courses in college and learned the little I know on the job."

"No better place to learn than on the job! Look, the way I see it is you've been in the minor leagues over there in Hartford. You've got some good experience under your belt. But now, it's time to move up to the majors. How'd you like to work for us at UST?"

Speechless, I could only stare, my mouth hanging open.

"We're adding to our *Exclusive News* teams in our owned and operated stations in Chicago, DC, LA. Where would you like to go?"

"I, uh ... I don't know what to say."

"I recommend Los Angeles. I think you'll do well on the west coast. It has a large, growing Latino demographic."

Numbness seeped into my bones. I tried to stand. "Mr. Cousins, I need to talk things over with my wife."

"A wise decision," said Mr. Cousins. "But I want you to meet the news team in our Hollywood studio first, as a courtesy to them, you understand. Have you ever been to LA?"

"No, sir."

"You'll love it, trust me."

"To tell you the truth, sir, I've always wanted to visit."

"It's where dreams are made," said Mr. Cousins, smiling and punching the intercom. The secretary picked up right away.

"Yes. sir?"

"We need to get a round-trip ticket to Los Angeles for Luis Rivera."

"For when, sir?"

"This afternoon," said Mr. Cousins, taking in my surprise with no reaction of his own.

"And the return flight?"

"Bring him back in a couple of days."

"Very well, sir."

"Mr. Cousins!" I interjected as he clicked off the intercom. "I can't go this afternoon. I don't have a change of clothes ... I ... I've just enough money for the train fare back to Hartford."

"It's a lot to happen all at once, I know. But don't worry. We'll give you some expense money and take care of the rest." He stood and offered his hand. "Welcome to the team."

I told Norma about the whirlwind swirling around me and that I would see her and the baby in a couple of days. I then explained to WHNB that an emergency required me to travel out of state for a few days. Within the hour, I was on my way to Kennedy Airport to catch a flight to LAX. My adrenaline pumped, and my excitement soared off the charts. Everything was moving too fast and took on a surreal sensation.

It was a five-hour flight to Los Angeles, but I gained three hours with the difference in time zones. I departed the airport and stepped into the bright sunshine. A limousine driver picked me up at the airport and drove me to Universal Studios Hotel in Hollywood. I checked into my room and, with nothing scheduled until the following morning, I decided to tour Universal Studios and a bit of Hollywood.

Universal Studios had been the stage of Lucile Ball and Desi Arnaz of the "I Love Lucy" television show. It was my mom's favorite sitcom and most of America's at the time. Among the outdoor attractions a self-proclaimed psychic gathered quite a crowd. I stayed in the background, watching as he called people out of the audience at random. After telling them about their past, he proceeded to declare what they should expect in the future. As the show ended and the crowd dispersed, I approached him even though I wasn't convinced of his psychic ability.

"Excuse me."

"Yes?"

"I'm about to start a new job and—"

"Hold it right there," he interrupted. "You weren't supposed to tell me that. I was going to tell you."

"Sorry."

"Anyway, go ahead."

"Yeah, well, I'm getting a new job soon and everything looks good, but—"

"It's a promotion, isn't it?"

"Yes, that's right! A big promotion."

The psychic looked at me keenly. "You're going to be successful. Everything's going to be fine."

"Is there more?"

"What else do you want to know?"

"How can you be so sure?"

The psychic shrugged. "It's what I do for a living. Good luck to you," he said, turning to walk away.

The sun still shone, but my stomach told me it was dinnertime. I had a pocketful of cash, so I treated myself to a nice meal at one of Hollywood's legendary restaurants, Musso & Frank Grill. With its wood-paneled walls and red-leathered mahogany booths, I felt I had taken a step back in time. Older waiters with bright red jackets served patrons (one of whom I could swear was Marlon Brando) at nearby tables.

What am I doing here? I took a sip of white wine and answered my own question. *I'm being called to the major leagues.*

Who would think that a *jibarito* from Santa Isabel, born in a tiny house built on stilts and who had grown up in the inner city of America, would have an opportunity like this?

After dinner, I went for a long walk. The balmy air and palm trees sang to me in my native tongue, as the evening breezes blew through the canyons. I found my way to the Walk of Fame along Hollywood Boulevard and stumbled upon the inlaid stars honoring famous motion picture, stage, and recording artists. I passed Grauman's Chinese Theater as though under a spell.

Young, strong, and bound for success, I wanted to run down the sidewalk and dance my own rendition of Gene Kelly's "Singing in the Rain" but was afraid of what people would think.

Later, I took a taxi back to the hotel and tried to sleep, but slumber slipped out of reach. My entire world had been turned upside down in fewer than twenty-four hours. Would that prove to be a good or a bad thing? I didn't bother to search for an answer. I stretched out on the bed and stared up at the ceiling, clenching my fists, trying to keep from screaming with joy at the top of my lungs.

Sometime well after midnight, I caught the classic movie *White Heat* on TV, starring James Cagney as a psychotic gangster who blows himself up at the end of the film.

"Made it, Ma! Top of the world!" he screamed just before the explosion.

LIVING BETWEEN CULTURES

Chapter 23

HOLLYWOOD SHOW BIZ

When I arrived at the Hollywood studio complex that housed the newsroom the following morning, the activity overwhelmed me. It was like being in a three-ring circus! Game-show participants whipped into a frenzy before going on-air were giddy at the prospect of winning a new car or a vacation to Hawaii. On the other side of the lot, actors and actresses prepared for the videotaping of soap operas and sitcoms.

The newsroom, tucked away in an area of its own, overflowed with writers, producers, reporters, and every want-to-be in between. There I met the management team.

I hit it off right away with Sam Passarelli, the general manager of KUST-TV, due in no small part to his being a New Yorker who made me feel right at home. It was a different story with Steve Johnson, the news director, and his top assistants Barry Acuff, assistant news director, and Doug Haley, news editor. They seemed to be giving me the cold shoulder. Like *papas sin sal* (potatoes without salt), they were humorless and strictly business with no warmth or accent to their speech, nothing spontaneous or colorful to connect them to a distinct part of the country or an ethnic group. I got a particularly cold vibe from Steve.

"I want you gentlemen to know I'm aware I'm the rookie here. I realize I need to prove myself."

"Don't you worry about a thing," said Sam. "We got you covered."

"I just want to be honest with all of you," I continued. "I know I have my weak spots, and there is always room for improvement. I tried to tell that to Mr. Cousins."

Sam waved his hands at me in a familiar New York gesture indicating it was of little consequence and I was not to worry. "We have plenty of producers and writers to help you," he said. And you'll get a lot of support around here." He looked at Steve and the others. "Isn't that so, fellas?"

I wished I had a camera. The grim faces of Steve and his two assistants spoke a thousand words. I tried to put myself in Steve's shoes. He probably felt like the baseball manager who gets a new player from the club's farm team and is expected to put him in the rotation when he could have hired a seasoned veteran. In other words, I was a bother to him. I didn't know what corporate politics were being played between LA and New York, but I represented a risk he didn't want to take, and it was being forced on him. Whatever he might be thinking, if I should take the job with KUST, I would have to keep my guard up around him.

Sam swung his arm around my shoulder. "C'mon, Lou, let's take you on a quick tour of the studio, and then I want you to go see Simon."

"Simon?"

"He's the color consultant for our tailor. You'll be getting three or four custom-made dress jackets with our logo to use on air."

I rubbed my forehead, exhaling deeply. "This is all so unreal," I said. "I haven't even accepted the job."

"You're gonna turn all this down?" asked Sam with a smile. He gestured around the cavernous work area, ironically called the "bullpen," where each reporter had his cubicle, and people were rushing madly back and forth. "This is where it's at, man!"

"I understand, Sam, but I need to talk things over with my wife."

After a whirlwind of meetings, I finally met with Simon at his exclusive shop in Beverly

Hills. He finished taking my measurements and, as it was nearing five o'clock, invited me to accompany him to his favorite *cantina* in Marina Del Rey.

While driving down the 405 Freeway, a large, elegant bearded man pulled beside us driving an older, white Rolls Royce convertible. I did a double-take.

"Is that Orson Welles in the Rolls?" I asked.

Simon glanced over and nodded. "Sure is."

"That's the writer and star of the movie classic, Citizen Kane!"

"He usually rides around in an ambulance," said Simon.

"An ambulance? I didn't know he was sick."

"He's not sick. He uses the ambulance to get from one film set to another in a hurry." Simon stole another look. "He doesn't seem to be in a rush tonight."

I couldn't believe my eyes. Orson Welles, the former husband of Latina actress, Rita Hayworth (*Margarita Carmen Cansino*), in a Rolls Royce right next to me!

Wait until I tell Norma!

Marina Del Rey boasted an upscale setting with an exclusive marina and wide streets lined with majestic palms and shade trees. Simon pulled up to a Polynesian-style restaurant/bar, and we walked in to find happy hour in progress.

Before I could reach the bar to order a drink, two young women grabbed me, one on each arm.

"He's mine!" said the blonde, pulling my right arm.

"No, I grabbed him first!" said the other, a curvaceous brunette.

I stared at the two of them, speechless. Were these the California girls I had heard of? Simon laughed, inViting everyone to a round of drinks. I held out my arms to the two of them, and we walked together to the bar. An hour later and several drinks later, my head spun. I skipped dinner, but the drinking continued. Simon offered to drive me back to my hotel around 8 PM, but I wasn't ready to go. The night was young and so was I. There was some partying left in me, and I wanted to enjoy every minute of this mini-vacation.

I woke up around 5 AM, still on East Coast time.

What a splitting headache! My second thought quickly followed the first. *Where am I?*

I couldn't remember how I got to the hotel or what happened after drinking the last tequila shot. I didn't see anyone beside me in the bed.

What happened last night?

I took a shower, packed my things, and strode to the door hoping I wouldn't miss my flight. My head still ached.

On the return to New York, I considered all that occurred during my short trip to LA. There was a lot at stake not only professionally but for my family. I absent-mindedly rubbed my fingers along my shirtsleeves.

My cufflinks are missing.

I had left them on the nightstand in the hotel room. Everything was moving too quickly and, as I had been careless with my cufflinks, I hoped I would not lose my confidence, identity, and family as a result of this move to the west coast of America.

Chapter 24

TRANSITIONS

Norma excitedly plied me for information about the trip. I didn't say much apart from telling her that the offer to work at KUST was a legitimate dream job with twice the salary and benefits.

Secretly, I had misgivings. I had received compliments on my television presence, how I came across as professional and caring, but beneath my neat appearance and business suits, I grappled with self-doubt. I had grown up poor. Though I spoke two languages, I sometimes felt I lacked command of either one. I had based my very start as a television news reporter on the credo "Fake it 'til you make it." In short, my foundations were weak, and I knew appearances could be deceiving.

Norma and I spent the next several days discussing the pros and cons of the various options before us. We were not eager to move so far away from family and the comfort of our surroundings, but the upside was too attractive to ignore. When I received a verbal promise from UST that I would be given additional training and support, I agreed to take the job. I should have made sure this promise was in the contract, but I didn't. This turned out to be a novice's inexperience that would come back to haunt me.

The news broke that I was going to Hollywood amid mixed reactions. Some co-workers at WHNB-TV were not as enthused as Moses about my receiving the offer. They had much more experience than I but hadn't been as fortunate. No doubt, there were those who saw my good fortune as an affirmative action move on the part of UST, even though they already had plenty of minority reporters.

UST's corporate leadership wanted to repeat the successes they had enjoyed under Adam Cousins' management and saw me as a good addition to his team. After all, Cousins knew how to pick a winner. I only needed a little more real-world experience along with a few breaks. Who knew? I might receive a major award of my own one day!

Most people in Hartford's Latino community seemed genuinely excited at our news and organized a farewell banquet that included speeches and a presentation of plaques.

There was also almost tangible disappointment on the part of some in the community that a young, homegrown activist with potential for political leadership was moving away. I was certain María Sanchez, one of my mentors, felt that way. She was very active as the leader of many organizations involving Puerto Ricans in Hartford and across Connecticut. While I was a college student, she and my old friend Andy Vazquez were instrumental in helping me become the youngest person, at that time, to lead the statewide Puerto Rican Day parade as its Grand Marshall. She and local social worker, Esther Jimenez, had been like civic and political *madrinas* (godmothers) to me. Our farewell was an emotional one.

Up until the last moment, I was tempted to back out. But the job in L.A. represented an opportunity to further my horizons and stretch my wings. If I didn't take the position, I might look back years later and wonder what I had missed. In the end, with my videographer Moses' prodding, I seized the moment and took the job at KUST. Norma, baby Danny, and I uprooted our family from Newington to re-locate three thousand miles away to the City of Angels.

City of Seduction would have been a more appropriate moniker. One of my first stories was to report on a police raid in a basement near the Hollywood strip. A cavernous sadomasochism club had been refurbished to look like a dungeon, replete with whips and shackles on the wall. I reported, still in shock at what I was seeing, with police moving about in the background. This was not a movie set; this was the real world I had contracted to work in.

Watching the newscast later that night, Norma was as taken aback as I had been. As streetwise inner-city kids, we hadn't missed much growing up, but consensual human bondage and ritual punishment with whips were foreign to us. In truth, the tawdry sexual subculture of Los Angeles went deeper than either of us could have imagined.

A few months after our arrival, Norma and I attended a cocktail party at a penthouse suite on Sunset Boulevard. One table offered a lavish spread of gourmet food and hors d'oeuvres, while another table displayed bowls of illicit drugs—a buffet for the indulgent. We pretended not to notice. A well-dressed couple approached us and introduced themselves in a friendly manner. I breathed a sigh of relief, thankful to finally meet someone who appeared to have a pleasant attitude and wasn't too strange.

After some small talk, the man remarked in a casual, unabashed manner, "In a little while we're going to have a party at our house, and we'd like to invite you and your lady."

"You mean when this party is over everyone will go to your house?" I asked.

"Actually," said the guy, taking a sip of his martini. "We were thinking of just having you and your lady."

I laughed. "That won't be much fun, will it?" I looked around the crowded room. "There're a lot of people here tonight. Don't you want to invite others? The more the merrier, they say."

"Yes, they do say that," said the man, chuckling in an odd sort of way. "But we were thinking of something more intimate."

"More intimate?"

"Yes. You can spend the evening with my lady, and I'll take yours. We'll have a lot of fun."

"What?!" I put my arm around Norma. "Look, man, this lady is my wife. Thanks, but no thanks. We're not into that sort of thing."

The man and his companion raised their eyebrows, gave us a curious look, and walked away.

I turned to Norma. "Do you believe what just happened?"

Norma shook her head, and we chuckled like children trying to mask their embarrassment.

Life wasn't always so strange, of course. We bought a nice one-story house in the San Fernando Valley and befriended regular people.

Except for the smog, we enjoyed the spectacular weather. I loved being able to drive from the Pacific coastline to the nearby mountains and from sandy beach to snow-capped peaks in the wintertime. We found the dry climate enjoyable, especially at night. Undeniably, there was something magical about southern California. Working at UST studios only amplified the mystique.

One moment I might be interviewing a national political leader like Secretary of State Henry Kissinger and the next moment find myself in the presence of A-list Hollywood stars like Mario Moreno, known as *Cantinflas*, the great Mexican actor whose movies I had loved and admired so much as a child.

My greatest thrill came from getting to know the personal side of some of these celebrities, who included my favorite Latin musicians like Tito Puente and Willie Bobo. I learned that celebrities have the same needs and vulnerabilities as everyone else. While their talents have been discovered and they are dedicated to their craft, they must work hard to ride the wave of public acceptance for as long as they can.

My hours were long and the work often dangerous and grueling. After being out in the field most of the day covering stories firsthand, I had to put in more hours back at the studio. Once, while covering a story at a murder scene in a housing project in the San Fernando Valley, my crew and I were nearly attacked by a gang of youth angered that I tried to interview witnesses.

On another occasion, we were nearly engulfed by a fire that suddenly broke out as we were reporting on a crashed jetliner. My colleagues probably wished for the adrenaline high of reporting about a catastrophe every day of the week and being first on the scene for an exclusive report. Not me! Being a people person, a feeler, I cared about the average people on the street and enjoyed interacting with them, not having to report on the gruesome side of life and walking by charred or blood-splattered human anatomy. The odor of death and visions of corpses affected my sleep and view on life. The joy of working in my chosen career quickly faded.

The newsroom politics one had to play troubled me, along with the high rate of turnover among personnel. There seemed to be a revolving door of new faces popping up every six months. Before long even the most seasoned reporters wondered if they would be forced to move to a remote, smaller market in search of employment.

Ironically, I grew increasingly popular among a growing segment of KUST's demographic—the Latino community in southern California. I wasn't afraid to cover a story with Spanish-speaking people. I spoke to them in Spanish and provided a spontaneous translation in English for viewers at home. Not a familiar scene in those days. I closed my reports by pronouncing my name with a Spanish accent the way it was intended to be spoken. Latino viewers loved these touches because they showed sensitivity and respect for our culture. But the admiration wasn't mutual from Steve and his inner circle.

"We aren't a Spanish-speaking station here, Rivera. They've got their own outlets for that stuff," he said in his deep, intimidating voice.

He wasn't the only one unhappy with my speaking Spanish on air. Occasionally, mail would arrive bearing the signature of a white-supremacist group like the Ku Klux Klan telling me to, "Go back to where you came from!" A complaint from a Latino embarrassed by my imperfect Spanish hurt the most. My Spanglish wasn't good enough.

I wasn't the only one having problems coping with the pressures of Hollywood. Another Puerto Rican, much more famous than I, experienced his own difficulties at another studio across town.

Chapter 25

BORICUAS IN L. A.

Freddie Prinze, a comedic genius and star of the sitcom *Chico and the Man*, gained instant stardom in his late teens after his debut on the *Tonight Show* with Johnny Carson. Once he started earning a star's income, Freddie purchased a house in the San Fernando Valley and arranged for his parents to move from their home in New York City.

Tony, an old friend of Norma's parents, lived in LA and did some of the electrical work at Freddie's parents' house. Tony arranged a date for us to meet. We hit it off immediately. Freddie's parents, María and Karl Pruetzel, brought with them a sorely missed touch of the Bronx and Puerto Rico, and an enduring friendship began.

Freddie rarely visited his parents because of his busy schedule, and I became an adopted son of the family. Seeing María was like visiting my own mother. She had that wonderful Puerto Rican accent that Freddie would joke about in his comedy routines.

During my frequent visits to the Pruetzel home, I learned more of the terrible pressures Freddie lived under. Performance schedules challenged even the most seasoned artists and managers, let alone a young man barely out of his teens. In addition to the taping of his television show in Burbank, he might also be shooting a movie, recording a comedy record, or flying to Las Vegas to perform live in front of huge audiences.

Watching things unfold from a distance, I hated seeing him suffer such relentless pressure. I knew from conversations with his parents that they, too, were very concerned. They felt his marriage had been hasty to say the least. Then Freddie began taking prescription drugs to cope with the strains of his hectic schedule.

However, the man on the street could not be blamed for thinking of Freddie as one of the happiest people on the planet. He was certainly one of the most popular! Who knows? Did he thrive on all the stress in his life to feed his comedy routines? Or was he laughing on the outside and crying on the inside? Or perhaps both?

I spoke with him on several occasions, but the short phone calls were limited to conversations about meeting at his parents' home or participating in Hispanic community events. It was my way of reaching out to let him know there was a fellow Boricua who wanted to connect with him and be a friend.

During one such conversation, I invited him to join me and several *salsa* music bands on a holiday show for Latinos at a prison in nearby Chino. Freddie's first reaction was to tell me how he appreciated the invitation and that, if it had been under different circumstances, he would have participated.

"But I can't do it Louie," he went on to say. "My manager would never let me put on a show in a prison." With a chuckle, he continued, "If the inmates had a riot, they'd take me hostage, and I'm too young to die, man."

"I understand, Freddie. Don't worry about it. Hope to see you soon. Take care."

That Mother's Day, Norma, Danny, and I dropped by María's house in the late afternoon. We brought a bouquet of flowers for María, as well as a pot of *asopao de pollo* (chicken and rice stew) Norma had prepared. María loved the flowers, while Karl seemed pleased with the stew.

When I asked María if Freddie would be visiting, her mood altered.

"He couldn't make it," she sighed. "Something came up."

"The price of success," I said, trying to take Freddie's side somewhat. "I know he would want to be here."

The conversation changed as María focused her attention on Danny. I picked up an open book laying on the coffee table. It was Maria's Bible. My eyes fell on a verse she had underlined,

"The righteous perish, and no one takes it to heart; the devout are taken away, and no one understands that the righteous are taken away to be spared from evil."

"Isaiah 57:1," I read aloud. I noticed a date written beside the verse: 9th May 1976.

That's today's date, I thought.

Additional notes and comments were written in the margins. I turned the pages and saw that most of Maria's Bible was marked up.

"Hey, María," I said. "What's all this writing in your Bible? You're gonna get the priest mad at you. Isn't writing in the Bible some kind of sin?"

María laughed. "God wants us to read the Bible. Didn't you know that, Louie?"

I laughed. "I don't know if I believe everything written in the Bible."

"It wouldn't hurt you to read it." Norma shook her head. "Everyone should read the Bible. Freddie reads his Bible all the time. And when I get a special word or insight, I make a note in the margin."

I set the book back on the coffee table. It felt hot in my hands. "What's so special about today?" I asked.

"It's Mother's Day," said Norma.

"Yeah, I know that." Then I turned and looked at María. "I mean what's so special that you wrote down today's date next to chapter fifty-seven of ... what was it called? Isaiah ..."

Everyone turned to María, but before she could say anything, a loud noise came from the kitchen as though something metal had fallen on the floor. I looked around. Danny was missing.

"Danny!" I shouted. "Where are you?"

"Dad!" chirped Danny from the kitchen. Then something else clanged. Norma ran into the kitchen followed closely by María.

"Don't worry about it," said María. "He probably just got into the pots and pans."

María picked up Danny and I smiled. Here, at least for a moment, life made some sense. A measure of sanity had been restored, short lived though it might be.

The righteous are taken away to be spared from evil, I thought, recalling what the

Bible verse had said. That certainly wasn't written for me.

Chapter 26

ENOUGH!

Several months later, while working at my desk at the KUST studios, I got a call from a Latino newspaper reporter who alerted me to a situation needing wider media exposure. An unlicensed doctor was running a makeshift clinic out of a house to help undocumented Latina women with the delivery of their infants.

"Tell me more."

"He's charging $250 for each baby he delivers."

"But what choice do these women have?" I asked, still not seeing the news angle. "Without papers, they could be deported."

"Babies are dying, Luis. Do you understand? The guy's bad news. If a woman has complications and requires a C-section, he's not licensed to perform surgery. The woman ends up being rushed to the hospital in an ambulance. And, allegedly, thirteen or more babies have already died."

"That's got to stop."

"You're tellin' me, but nobody's paying any attention. You know the majority doesn't do anything about issues concerning people of color until it starts affecting them."

"Who is this guy?"

"I know where you can find him, and I'm sure you'll raise awareness if you do a report. The entire country needs to see what this guy's doing."

With the news editor's permission, I pulled a crew together and went out to investigate. I knew in my gut that I finally had a story I could sink my teeth into as a reporter. It felt good. I was returning to my roots of social activism, of helping people and speaking up for those who didn't have a voice. This was a story that had the potential to save lives.

When we arrived at the doctor's house in the foothills of the San Gabriel Mountains, we opened the door, cameras rolling. A half-dozen or so female patients lay on army-type cots spread all over the place. Seeing me, the videographer and soundperson, they panicked and tried to get out of their cots to hide.

"¡No se apuren! ¡No estoy aquí para hacerles daño!" ("Don't worry! I'm not here to harm you!")

Hearing me speak to them in Spanish calmed them down a little, but they continued looking around in fear and consternation. I had seen that look many times before. I called out again to reassure them.

"Estoy aqui para ayudarles." ("I'm here to help you.") Just then, a nurse's aide stalked up to me.

"What are you doing here?" she asked. "What do you want?"

"I understand you're running some kind of maternity clinic here," I said, pointing the microphone toward her.

"That's right."

"It's been reported several women have lost their babies because your medical director can't perform C-sections."

"No, no ... we're trying to help is all."

"Are babies dying, ma'am?"

Just then, the doctor came in. A Caucasian man, probably in his mid-thirties, with thinning hair and glasses, he wore a wrinkled white jacket over his button-down shirt. "How may I help you?" he asked.

"I'm Luis Rivera from *Exclusive News.* Do you have a license to run this clinic?"

"I'm not doing anything wrong here," said the doctor, glancing around nervously. "I'm helping these ladies. They have nowhere else to go."

"Except to the emergency room if you botch the delivery of their baby or if they need a C-section which you can't perform!"

"No, you got it all wrong. You can't just come barging in here like this!" He glowered at my videographer and soundperson. "We're trying to provide a service. What do you want from me?"

I held firm, improvising and asking questions for another ten minutes or so as the videographer did his thing. I managed to speak with some of the women who had been attending the clinic, while I spontaneously translated their remarks. One woman burst into tears, saying she was scared and had nowhere else to go. She feared for her life and that of her unborn child.

Later in the day, after returning to the studio, I got a surprise phone call from a representative of the authorities handling the case.

"Mr. Rivera, we need to ask you to keep your story of the doctor under wraps for now. We've been working on this case for some time, and we're almost ready to move in. Can you keep your story off the air a little longer?" He spoke in a somber tone.

"I don't know. I'll have to get the News Director's permission," I said. "About how long?"

"A few days or so. We're really close to arresting this guy."

"Let me see what I can do," I said.

"Thank you, sir."

I went to see Steve and told him about the situation. He listened carefully and nodded. "Give me the video, and we'll let you know when the story breaks."

Though it was what I wanted to hear, I was surprised to hear it just the same.

Maybe Steve isn't as bad a guy as I thought.

I left the office feeling great, especially since Steve didn't yell my name across the bullpen telling me to stay and work overtime. Things were looking up. I knew from experience that one good break could set a person on an entirely new course in life.

A few days later, I was at home watching my station's evening news, as I often did to see what tips I could learn from other reporters. A feature story appeared on a doctor arrested in the deaths of several infants.

Wait a minute. That sounds like my story.

And it was! But another reporter (an older, Anglo man) signed out with his name. There was little mention of my involvement. I could feel my blood pressure throbbing in my temples. I was not going to keep quiet about my displeasure.

The following morning, I marched into Steve's office. "I need to talk with you," I said.

"Yeah, what do you need?" he replied in his deep, former announcer's voice.

"I think you already know," I said, taking a seat in front of him.

"Why don't you enlighten me, Rivera?"

"No, why don't you enlighten me?"

"I suppose you're referring to the scoop on the clinic," he said, leaning back in his chair and cupping his hands behind his head.

"That was *my* story!"

"Correction, Rivera. It's *our* story, the station's story. Everything you do belongs to us. You know that."

"But why didn't you tell me you were going to air it. You promised to let me finish it."

"You were in the field, and it was best to let Marvin close for you."

"Why did this new guy need to close for me? It was my report!" I stood and glared down at Steve. "Look, you haven't liked me from the moment I walked into this place. Why don't we just call it for what it is? You can have your job. I quit!"

"You can't quit. You're under contract. The only way you can leave is if you're fired," replied Steve with a smirk.

He was right; the contract was specific. But it didn't matter. I turned to leave.

"I'm outta here. I'm finished with this mind game."

I returned to my desk and packed my stuff. As I walked across the bullpen toward the exit, I found myself anticipating Steve making one last sarcastic comment. But it never happened. All I could hear was the hum and buzz of the worker bees. For the first time in months, I got home in time for dinner.

The next day, I got a call from the studio manager, Sam Passarelli. "Hey, Lou, what happened with you and Steve?"

"You really want to know what happened?"

"Yeah, I want to know."

"Sam, here I am, thousands of miles from home. I had a good job in Connecticut. I was growing in my craft, getting better all the time, respected in my community. And I come to the West Coast thinking I'm going to improve, become a better reporter, and contribute to the community here. But I have to say I don't even know why you guys hired me."

"You're a good reporter, Lou. You got talent."

"Yet when I have an important report like this last one on the doctor, your guy takes it away from me! If I didn't know any better, Sam, I'd say there's some sort of discrimination going on."

"No way, Lou. I'd never allow that."

"Maybe not, but I can't say the same for some of the folks who work under you. I told you from the beginning I felt I needed some support and you promised I'd get it. But I got nothing. I had to nearly beg for some black-and-white fan photos." I paced back and forth, venting my frustration. "Nobody has ever taken a minute of their precious time to begin to show me the ropes. What's the deal, Sam? Was I just being set up for failure? Is that what's going on? I should sue you guys for not keeping your verbal promises."

"Now, come on, Lou. You don't need to talk like that. Look, why don't you take some time and let the dust settle."

"I can't work for that news director anymore, Sam. I just can't."

"Then I'll keep you on the payroll for, say, ten weeks, and we'll release you from the contract."

I thought of the ten weeks as a long-needed vacation. Completely burned out, I accepted Sam's offer.

Chapter 27

WHEN THE CITY OF ANGELS CRIED

My ten weeks on the KUST payroll passed too quickly, and I needed to earn some money fast. Television news was out of the question. There was no returning to that hard-news, pressure-cooker existence. It had already left me in a near nervous breakdown. I wanted to become like any other normal guy supporting his family. The business leads from friends and acquaintances didn't result in any promising income-generating opportunities, and I was desperate.

Like many job hunters, I searched the newspaper classified ads offering paid training for a new career. The ads that caught my eye were in sales. Insurance seemed like a decent opportunity that would provide immediate cash flow. I enjoyed helping others, and I remembered the compassionate and caring attitude of the insurance agent who had guided me through the steps following my younger brother Benjy's untimely death.

Norma knew I yearned to be self-employed, so she agreed with my joining a nationally known life insurance company and supported me fully when I departed for several days of training in Anaheim, California. I embraced my opportunity to have more flexibility and say-so in my work.

On Friday morning, a little after 7 a.m. the alarm clock radio blared.

"Actor Freddie Prinze, star of the hit television show *Chico and the Man*, was admitted to UCLA Medical Center earlier this morning suffering a gunshot wound to the head. His condition is listed as critical ..."

I shot out of the bed. My knees buckled, as I fell back on the edge of the mattress, staring at the radio in shock and disbelief. Panic seized my heart, as the newscaster's voice grew more and more distant, like someone shouting over the roar of a waterfall: *Police responded in the early morning hours ... Comstock Wilshire Hotel ... to the temple ... massive injury ...*

With trembling hands, I threw my clothes in a small suitcase, wondering how Maria and Karl were dealing with this nightmarish news.

My goal was to reach the hospital as quickly as possible. Calvin, my hotel roommate, appeared in the doorway of the bathroom, toweling his hair dry.

"What's up, brother?"

"You gotta cover for me," I said, rushing to the door.

"Why? What's happening?"

"Tell the trainer an emergency came up. I'll call later."

I was one of about a dozen trainees who had to undergo an intensive program on our way to becoming licensed agents. Today was the last day of our training, and I was tired. But this fatigue reached deeper than physical weariness and came from more than a lack of sleep.

I wasn't sure if I wanted to be an insurance salesman. The top salespeople participating in providing the training were totally focused on the dollar figures needed to ensure success. I wasn't that hard core. Financially, I had little choice, but that didn't keep me from feeling like a fish out of water. After all, I had moved to Hollywood from Connecticut two years earlier to be a hot-shot reporter for United States Television's (UST's) *Exclusive News* team.

Calvin put his hand on my shoulder. "You don't look so good, my man. You look like you're somewhere else. What's up?"

"It's a friend of the family," I said.

227

The radio announcer's voice pierced the momentary silence. *"Mr. Prinze's manager appears to have tried to get the gun away from the popular comedian, but was unsuccessful in his attempt ..."*

Calvin looked at the radio and then turned back to me, his mouth agape. "Freddie Prinze?"

I nodded. "It looks like he shot himself in the head." I opened the door and was gone.

I listened to the radio during the drive to the hospital and continued to gather information on the gut-wrenching news about Freddie. It was reported he had been despondent for weeks. In receipt of divorce papers from his wife of about a year, he was concerned about the custody of their baby boy. He had a revolver in his possession and had been seen playing with it over the last several days and pretended a few times around friends that he had been shot. A note was found in the apartment written in Freddie's own hand: "I must end it. There's no hope left. I'll be at peace."

It seemed contrary behavior for the confident young star I had the pleasure of speaking to on a few occasions.

I reached the hospital in less than an hour and pushed my way through the paparazzi to take the elevator to the Intensive Care Unit on one of the upper floors. As the doors opened, I saw María, Freddie's mother, sitting in a chair against a wall in the middle of the corridor, with Karl, her husband and Freddie's father. I started toward them. A security guard stopped me before I took two steps, but María stood to intervene.

"It's okay. Let him go!" she cried in a hoarse voice. "He's family!"

The security guard backed away, and I hurried toward María. I hugged her tightly as she spoke to me in Spanish, wiping away her tears, "Louie, come here. Look what they've done to my son."

The anguish in her voice confirmed my worst fears: Freddie was fighting for his life. I followed her into the room where Freddie lay on the bed, his head bandaged, his body connected to a life-support machine. My first impression of him lying there so thin and frail looking was that of Jesus hanging on the cross.

There were others in the room: his estranged wife; television producer Ray Andrade; singer and television star Tony Orlando; and the actor Isaac Ruiz (who had a recurring role as Mando in *Chico and the Man*). They knew me as Luis Rivera, news reporter for KUST's *Exclusive News*. I didn't bother telling them I had quit my job several months earlier.

For the rest of the day and into the night, phone calls from around the nation jammed the hospital's switchboard. People of all ages asked about Freddie's condition and offered their prayers for his recovery.

I called Norma, who just a week earlier had given birth to our second son, Benjamin. I counted on her to be very strong and on her own while I focused on Freddie's tragedy. I let her know I planned to stay in the hospital overnight. She had heard the news about Freddie like most of America and encouraged me to make myself available to help Karl and Maria in any way possible.

A little after seven in the morning, twenty-four hours since first hearing the tragic news, I was awakened by Maria. She asked me to drive Karl home, so he could take a shower and catch a brief nap. An hour or so later, I returned to the hospital, and María pulled me to one side.

"The doctors talked to me," she said. "Freddie don't have any brain activity. They want to know what the family wants to do."

"What do you mean, Maria?"

"They ask if we want to turn the machines off."

I took a moment to gather my thoughts. "I know you have a lot of faith. Are you sure this is the right thing to do?"

María looked at me with what I can only describe as profound sadness. "I have prayed and know that God can do miracles, but now he's calling Freddie home. I know I'll see him again." She put her hand on my face and added,

"I'm not giving up, Louie. I'm letting go. It's only the machine that's keeping Freddie alive."

I looked away, struggling to hold back my tears.

"I need you to pick up Karl," she continued. "But don't tell him what's going on. When he gets back, we'll let him know."

I pulled myself together and drove to the house in Van Nuys. I woke Karl. He took a shower and dressed slowly, putting on a three-piece suit and silk tie. Tall and porcelain-skinned, he looked like a member of an aristocratic European family. He showed little emotion, but I think he was numb with shock and grief. He combed his white hair straight back, made a final adjustment to his necktie, and lit up a cigarette, knowing he wouldn't be able to have one at the hospital. Neither of us said much, and I tried not to appear impatient, but I was afraid it might all be over by the time we got back to the hospital.

We returned to the ICU a little after one o'clock. María spoke with Karl, whose hands began to shake, and then a doctor walked out of Freddie's room. It was over. The life-support machinery was silent. Freddie was gone.

This all seemed too familiar. I felt as though I was reliving the moments during the summer of 1962 when Benjy lay lifeless at the funeral home with his head bandaged. I found it hard to breathe and, stumbling back, found a small chair in the room, and sobbed.

I wasn't related to Freddie, but I felt such a tremendous loss nonetheless, not only for his family but for all Puerto Ricans who had just lost a favorite son. Freddie was a talented *Boricua* with such great potential. Like much of the Latino community, I considered him a brother because he shared our community's culture and nuances in his humor. In addition, while I might not have known him well, I considered his mother as my second mother, and she considered me as a second son.

"He's going home," María had said. "I will see him again."

I did not have María's faith. I didn't even have Freddie's faith. María had told me Freddie knew and memorized Bible scriptures. He believed in God but had been overwhelmed by the pressures of being a star in Hollywood. He died at the age of twenty-two, barely even a man. Fame and fortune had been too much for him, too fast. That was what María had meant when she said, *"Look what they've done to my son."*

I could relate. My mother had said much the same thing to me a few months earlier during a brief visit from Puerto Rico. From her perspective, I was adrift in my search for success and prosperity, rudderless and without a moral compass. My pursuit of the American Dream had taken me on a rollercoaster ride. Now, numb, bewildered, and crying uncontrollably from grief and lack of sleep, I wanted desperately to get off the ride, but the ride wouldn't stop. In fact, it rolled faster and faster, turning everything in front of me into a blur of shame and remorse. There was a pounding in my head, and I imagined the beating of the surf in peaceful Santa Isabel, where I had been born.

Is this how the struggle for life in Hollywood ends? I wondered. *There was once a piece of paradise that I knew ... where the sea breezes caressed me at night and the morning dew kissed my cheek.*

Could that magical time be recaptured? Would it set me on the right course again? Clearly, something was missing in my life. I didn't know if it was something I had lost along the way or something I never had. I only knew my innermost being desperately needed *something*. I had to find *it* if it could be found.

Following Freddie's death (and Karl's death from lung cancer almost two years later), I continued to visit Maria to check on her and couldn't help but admire her remarkable faith. Freddie had left a small estate, and, after all the legal and other expenses were paid, there was little left for his family. The life insurance company would not pay the benefits on his policy because his death had been ruled a suicide by the coroner's office. María seemed to take it all in stride.

Whenever I visited her, she would be reading her Bible. If I asked her what plans she had for paying her bills, she would answer that everything was in God's hands, and He would provide for her needs. I questioned how she could maintain her faith considering all the tragedy she had experienced. Where did her deep assurance and peace come from? It was hard for me, a non-spiritual person, to understand. I honestly thought her grief was causing her to lose touch with reality.

I believed Maria needed salvation from her irrational religious beliefs, and I saw myself as on a mission to help her face life without dependence on an invisible God who might, or might not, exist. Her talk about relying on God to supply all her needs seemed to be a lot of wishful thinking. I saw her as alone and vulnerable, much as my mother had been at times when I was young. I desperately wanted to help Maria but didn't know how.

One evening I shared my concerns about her radical Christian beliefs and tried to sell her on how she needed some happiness in life.

"Maria, you need to move on and stop surrounding yourself with all of these pictures and memorabilia of Freddie. This place looks like a sanctuary. You need to do something that will bring happiness in your life."

I pulled out a joint and offered it to her. It was the best marijuana I could find. Maria stared at me in disbelief.

"What is it you young people find so good about this stuff?" she asked in her heavy Puerto Rican accent.

"It makes you feel happy, María. It lets you forget about your worries."

"Feel happy?"

With unabashed confidence, I continued trying to convince her to share the joint with me. "This is how I relax. It changes your mood and makes you want to laugh your problems away."

Without hesitation, and like a warrior ready to do battle, María looked into my glassy eyes and said emphatically, "My body is the temple of the Holy Spirit, Louie, and nothing is going to change that. What you need in *your* life is Jesus Christ!"

"Jesus Christ?!' I blurted.

"He'll change your life if you'll let Him."

"Hang on, María. I don't think you understand. I'm trying to help you. All this prayer and Bible reading ... you're losing touch with the real world."

"The real world where you place your loyalties, Louie, the world you live in ... the body you inhabit ... that 'world' is short lived and passes away. Set your priorities straight, *mijo*! It's your spirit that lives forever."

I had not expected María's response. The whole discussion about spirits was too spooky for me, and I told her I had to go home. I had gone to her house to set her straight, but the script had been flipped, and I was the one on the defensive.

When I returned home that night, I found a package of letters forwarded to me from KUST. Even though I no longer worked in television, fan mail still arrived for me periodically. One particular letter was from a woman named Suzy, whom I had met while I was a news reporter. She had invited me to speak to gang members as part of a community outreach program.

At the time, Suzy had her own troubles and struggled to raise several children as a single parent. But as her letter now recounted, she had since met a good man named Ron. They had married, and she was now a committed Christian. She described the blessings of her new and meaningful life, adding that she and her husband were praying for me to give Jesus a chance. Included in the envelope was a little Christian booklet that talked about "faith in the living Christ."

I couldn't believe what I was reading. First María and now Suzy. What made Christianity so special? As a young teen, after my little brother died, I believed God and His servants had let me down. How could I be expected to turn my life over to Jesus and become one of those fanatical believers? Luis Rivera a Pentecostal holy-roller? It didn't make sense to believe in something you couldn't see or touch.

Or did they know something I didn't know?

My insecurities worsened and so did our finances. Working by straight commission wasn't easy. I decided to take Maria, Suzy, and the author of that little tract up on their challenge to seek God. That night, while Norma and the boys were sleeping, I smoked some marijuana in the kitchen and worked up the courage to say out loud what was most on my heart and mind.

Looking up at the ceiling I blurted, "God ... if You can even hear me, I have a question for You. Why did You bring me all the way out here to LA, thousands of miles from my birthplace and extended family, just to let me fail so miserably? I'm not a bad person. All I ever wanted to do was help people and support my family."

Almost immediately, I received an answer. It didn't come in a booming audible voice; it came from within. A gentle, calm voice said, "When you give Me one-hundred percent of your love, I will take you away from all of this."

When I heard those words, everything made sense. It seemed like an invisible hand turned a special key and unlocked the heavy chains that had weighed me down my entire life. Someone had finally cut through the haze of my existence and realized I struggled with abandonment and not feeling truly loved or being able to provide real love. I broke down and wept like a lost child.

God was asking me for the kind of commitment we seek from someone we deeply love and who we want a personal relationship with. "Faking it till you make it" doesn't work with God. He wasn't asking me to give Him superficial lip-service or even the well-intentioned Christmas-and-Easter-inspired recognition the world gives. He wanted to be first in line for my affection. He wanted *all* my love.

In that moment, I realized a choice had to be made: either love Him or love the worldly motivations of fame, money, and the trappings of material success. Why? Because, as Maria had pointed out, our spirits live forever, and material things are like the grass of the field that flourishes one day and perishes the next. Through my tears, I asked for His forgiveness. I had a vision where I saw myself standing before thousands of people telling them of my love for my God ... the Father, Son (Jesus Christ), and Holy Spirit.

As a way of showing God that He now had my full attention, I picked up a pen and paper and wrote, "I am a minister of God's word" and signed my name. All I could do was cry as I repeated, "Oh, my God" over and over again. I hadn't cried that hard since Benjy died, and, again, when Freddie Prinze had passed away. I knew I would never again need to depend on drugs or deny my wife and children my love and full attention.

"So if the Son sets you free, you will be free indeed!" John 8:36 (ESV)

LIVING BETWEEN CULTURES

Chapter 28

CHANGING PERCEPTIONS OF TRUTH

Looking for answers, I shared my experience with every Christian I could find, beginning with María.

She gazed at me with her dark, brown eyes shining. "Now, you're my brother as well as my son!" she exclaimed, embracing me.

Apart from wanting to tell others about the great change I felt in my life, I also sought confirmation that what I had experienced that night in the kitchen was a spiritual awakening and not a drug-induced hallucination. God, always faithful, gave me one confirming sign after another that He had, indeed, taken me under His wing and shown me mercy.

After a meeting of Latino businessmen, I drove to a restaurant with a man who, my friend Alex Soto had told me, was a knowledgeable Christian believer. I wanted to ask his thoughts regarding my recent experience with God.

Before I began, he turned to me and said in an emotional voice, "Luis, God has impressed upon me to tell you that He wants you to be a minister of His Word."

How could he have known about my private commitment to God just a short while ago? I could do nothing but break into tears.

Over the next few months, I visited different churches until I discovered the Church on the Way, pastored by Dr. Jack Hayford. He had a gentle, easygoing way of communicating and possessed a vast knowledge of the Bible as well as a deep commitment to Christ. I felt at home there and decided to be baptized at his church.

Initially, Norma was happy to learn that I had made a commitment to change my old ways and had resolved to live a life focused on God and my family. But she wasn't at all impressed with the religious legalism and judgmental attitude that came with it, which was of my own making, a misguided practice some new Christians followed and never recover from.

Instead of demonstrating my love to my family by becoming the servant leader of my home and instead of patiently and kindly helping my spouse and children understand why I became a believer, in my ignorance I tried to shove my beliefs down their throats and became overbearing. In my haste, I unwittingly took scripture out of context instead of planting a seed and letting God do His work. Rather than a prayer of blessing and thanksgiving at the dinner table, I'd complain in pious tones about what Norma or the boys had done wrong that day.

This caused rebellion in our home. I meant well, yes, but I was far off base and driving Norma away through our arguments, rather than modeling God's love and acceptance to her.

The only thing I did well under the circumstances was to get on my knees in prayer and ask God for forgiveness and for His will to be done.

"I love Norma, Lord," I said one day in prayer. "This new life You've called me to isn't easy. It will never be all it's meant to be so long as she is on the outside looking in. Please help us, Father. Please work in the midst of this situation." Through prayer and discernment, I was able to understand my effect on those around me and determined to practice what I was preaching.

Norma worked for a private detective agency in downtown LA. Helen, a mature woman, owned the business next door, a company that did transcriptions and paralegal work for the detective agency. She often stopped in for work-related matters and developed a friendship with Norma. Observing the stream of undercover detectives and other men passing by Norma's desk and flirting with her incessantly, one day she spoke with Norma about the wonderful relationship she had with the most amazing man. Before long, she invited Norma and another co-worker to her home where she introduced them to this fantastic guy.

Helen's amazing guy was none other than her Lord and Savior, Jesus Christ. In Helen's home, Norma began to really study the Bible and pray. There she received an understanding of God's unconditional love and acceptance.

My spirit soared when, a few weeks later, she expressed the desire to go to church and began attending services with me regularly. One evening at an evangelistic meeting in Glendale, she heard a young Latino evangelist present the gospel. When he invited people to come forward to receive Christ as their Lord and Savior, to my surprise and without any prompting, Norma went forward unhesitatingly. Another miracle had occurred, and my marriage was being restored.

Around that time, I met Sonny Arguinzoni, the pastor of Victory Outreach Chapel. Sonny had been among the first of many ex-heroin addicts that evangelist Nicky Cruz helped convert to Christianity. Now Sonny was ministering to the youth gangs of East Los Angeles. I told Sonny about my conversion experience, and he mentioned that I should meet Nicky Cruz.

Cruz, born in Puerto Rico, was the former warlord of the infamous Mau-Mau gang in Brooklyn, New York. He became a Christian after a dramatic conversion during a revival meeting that had been expected to turn into a bloody gang war. His story was documented in the best-selling autobiography, *Run Baby Run,* and the movie *The Cross and the Switchblade.*

As it so happened, Suzy and Ron, who had been instrumental (along with María) in helping me come to Christ, planned to attend a meeting featuring Nicky Cruz near Disneyland in Anaheim, California. They invited me to join them. I didn't know what to expect, but I attended the event.

Nicky Cruz, dynamic in presenting his testimony, brought many to a closer relationship with God. I was excited to see this *Boricua* from the streets of New York, with his heavily accented English, being so well accepted by the audience. People clung to each word he said, straining to understand each word. I was moved when he spoke of Puerto Rico, his family, and what God had done in his life.

After preaching, he shook hands with those gathered, and I introduced myself. To my surprise he knew about my TV work and involvement with Freddie Prinze's parents. Before we parted, he asked me to visit him in his hotel room the next day. He wanted to make sure I understood how to learn more about my new walk with Christ.

We met the next day, and our conversation resulted in an invitation to join Nicky in a series of crusades in Venezuela. I didn't hesitate to accept the invitation. It seemed like something I was destined to do. I hungered to learn more about the faith that had changed my life so completely.

During the week or so we were in Venezuela, I witnessed many events that had no logical explanation. On several nights, dark storm clouds loomed over the Caracas stadium threatening rain. Stadium officials suggested that the meetings be postponed. Nicky and the sponsors refused, praying instead that God would intervene and save the thousands gathered from the torrential rains that appeared so imminent.

As the stadium personnel feared, the skies opened. Heavy rains poured over everything, the seats, the field, the stage. I didn't see how we'd be able to attract the audience needed to help defray the costs involved, but Nicky didn't seem worried. If he was, he did a good job hiding it.

Like María had done, Nicky would teach me to have faith. I quickly learned that even the united faith of a few could be a greater force than the doubts of many. Despite the weather forecast, over twelve thousand people gathered each night in the stadium to hear Nicky preach. Every time he approached the microphone, the rains would subside or completely stop, allowing him to address the crowd.

Despite all the potential problems that arose, there were great successes. Nicky's testimony touched the hearts of thousands of people, even though there were some who didn't want the gatherings to succeed. One evening, I was asked to share my love for Christ with the audience. Taken off guard, I blurted out a few sentences in broken Spanish. Though my words were not spiritually profound, the audience understood that I spoke from my heart and many seemed moved. The vision I had on that lifechanging night in my Los Angeles kitchen in which I had seen myself speaking before many people had become a reality.

After returning to LA, Nicky invited me and my family to join him on staff at his Colorado Springs ministry. It was hard to leave behind the friends Norma and I had shared so much joy and sorrow with over the previous years. What would happen to Maria and who would visit her like I had? Still, the peace in our hearts confirmed the move was for the best.

At a time when interest rates on home loans were in the double digits, our home sold immediately for almost three times what we had purchased it for. Nicky had previously told me not to worry, that God would help us with the sale of our home, and He did.

Chapter 29

MY FATHER'S SON

My involvement with the Nicky Cruz Outreach was my boot camp in Christianity. I felt like a raw recruit with a lot of questions and some lingering worldly habits. Nicky was like the drill instructor determined to get me into shape for spiritual battle. There's a saying, "*Old habits die hard.*" and it is largely true. But change really can happen when a personal relationship with God is established and discipleship is added to the picture. I deeply wanted to change my ways, and, even though I made a lot of mistakes, my heart was in the right place.

Nicky and his wife, Gloria, were true servants of God and helped me along my spiritual journey. They cared and prayed for my family and made a huge difference in our lives.

As I grew more stable emotionally and spiritually, I began to think of my larger family both in the States and in Puerto Rico. I had a strong desire to share with them my reconciliation with my faith.

My first inclination was to travel to Puerto Rico and spend time with Mom. In the back of my mind, there were also thoughts of Dad, who had retired from his job at the Inland Steel Mill and moved back to Borinquen where he remarried. I managed to say a few half-hearted prayers for him, but I didn't have a strong desire to visit. It was the wrong attitude for a believer to have, but, as I said earlier, *old habits die hard*.

My father had not attended Benjy's funeral, and I still resented him for that. Why would I want to see him? Of course, I knew the answer: I should want to see my father to make peace with him, to seek reconciliation, to share with him what I had seen and learned. It's easier said than done. The spirit was willing, but the flesh indeed was weak.

Mom was a different story. At the time, she and Daniel had built a home on the outskirts of Utuado, a town located north of Ponce in the mountainous western area of the island. Utuado had a rich history that included the presence of indigenous Taino people and the cultivation of coffee. The Tainos named the area *Otoao*,

"Between Mountains," but later it was renamed Utuado.

Utuado was the only place I had visited in Puerto Rico where I had to cover myself in bed with a blanket to warm the chilly nights. It also had abundant rainfall. Lush green hills surrounded my parents' home, and orange-red coffee berries, which at one time had been referred to as *Oro Negro* (black gold) dotted the valleys. My people love their *café con leche* (coffee and milk), and my parents became just as attached to the process of growing and cultivating their own "black gold."

I had been with Mom and Daniel for about five days when we learned that my biological father had been hospitalized with heart problems. I hesitated to go, but Mom had a *sentimiento* (feeling) that time was of the essence. We set out by car, navigating scary, hairpin turns that were a test for the bravest of souls and stomachs.

When we arrived at the hospital in Ponce and walked into Dad's room, we were struck by the frigid temperature. An eerie feeling washed over me when I touched his ice-cold skin. I learned later that the rooms were kept cold to help fight possible bacterial infections.

Suddenly, Dad's eyes opened, and he looked right at me. The sparkle in his eyes had dimmed. We couldn't engage in small talk, though we tried, because he had lost the ability to speak. Uneasily, I carried on a short conversation in English with my brother Guiso who sat in a chair beside our father's bed. As is customary in Puerto Rico, Guiso was the designated family member that stayed with the patient overnight. I really wanted to leave after a few minutes. I didn't hate my father, but the distance between us loomed.

Mom pulled me to the side and whispered in my ear something I never thought I would hear. Especially from her.

"Ask him to forgive you," she said.

"Forgive me?" I whispered back with a scowl.

"To forgive you for anything you may have said or done."

I was taken aback. Mom knew better than anyone the chasm that had been created in our relationship after Benjy died. What had I ever done to necessitate his forgiveness?

After a couple of minutes of mental jousting that culminated in the realization it was the right thing to do, I leaned down to my father's ear and said, *"Padre, perdóname si en algún momento te ofendí."* ("Father, forgive me if at any moment I offended you.")

To my great surprise, Dad moved one arm and pointed toward his chest. I didn't understand at first. I looked over at Mom. She had tears in her eyes, and I got it. Dad was trying to tell me that he wanted me to forgive him.

Speechless, I could only smile and nod, putting my hand over my heart to let him know I understood what he was trying to say. I reached down to kiss him, and the cold of that hospital room melted away with the warm sensation radiating from my heart and his.

He died of a heart attack a few days later. While I sorrowed for his passing, I also experienced joy that I had heeded my dear mother's advice and sought forgiveness. Mom always did have a sixth sense about such things.

Maybe at that moment in time we all sought forgiveness from one another. It needed to be done, especially since I professed to be a Christian. The reward was greater than I had anticipated. For years the resentment toward my father had festered in me and perhaps had caused me not to be as loving a husband and father as I could have been. Like having my sins forgiven when I asked Christ to forgive me, finally, I was at peace with my father. This dark cloud hanging over me evaporated. What kind of a Christian would I be if I could not ask for forgiveness? That unrepentant spirit could only disrupt my relationship with God and any blessings to follow.

Before returning to the States, I walked along the beach near *El Cocal* where I had been born. The waves washed ashore, and the breeze blew through my hair as I thought of the man who had been old enough to be my grandfather when I was born. He had been a *jíbaro*, a humble working man of the soil, and he went north to the mainland United States in search of a better tomorrow. In some respects, he achieved what he set out to do. By moving to the States and working hard, he gave me and his other children an opportunity to live the American Dream.

I was the first in my immediate family to attend a four-year college. I had been part of a movement to bring about needed social change in my community during a tumultuous time in American history, and I had achieved a measure of success in broadcast journalism. Most importantly, I had discovered that the greatest achievement of all is to know and love God and serve and honor Him with all my heart and soul.

Am I really that different from my father? I wondered. I, too, was a *jíbaro*, an AmeRICAN *jíbaro,* if you will, from humble roots who valued family, friends, community, and my faith. With tears in my eyes and after a lifetime of thinking I had little in common with my biological father, I came to realize we had more in common than I had believed.

I paused and gazed out at the beautiful sea, sparkling with waves of gold in the late afternoon. I would return to the States in a few days, but a piece of my heart would forever remain in Borinquen. I prayed that when my time would come to fall asleep and leave this world as my father had done, I might awaken to find a place of beauty not too far removed from the place I walked in now.

May it be so, I said to myself, singing those timeless verses from Puerto Rico's anthem written by Manuel Fernandez Juncos.

La Borinqueña

(translated by L. A. Rivera Colón)

> *The land of Borinquen*
> *where I was born.*
> *It is a flowering garden*
> *of magical brilliance.*
> *A sky always clean*
> *serves as a canopy.*
> *And placid lullabies are given*
> *by the waves at her feet.*
> *When at her beaches Columbus arrived,*
> *he exclaimed full of admiration:*
> *Oh! Oh! Oh!*
> *This is the beautiful land that I seek.*
> *It is Borinquen the daughter,*
> *the daughter of the sea and the sun ...*
> *the sea and the sun!*

My song finished, I walked back toward the *pueblo* of Santa Isabel, turning for a final glimpse of the white sand and aquamarine sea beyond. I listened to the soothing waves breaking along the shore and wanted to return somehow to that magical time when my mother had walked this same shoreline, singing, and speaking to me during her pregnancy. Of course, I knew that could never be. But there was a heaven yet to come and many reunions still to hold, and, in the grand scheme of things, I knew that time could not be very far away.

I wondered if heaven might not be so far removed from this enchanted island the *jíbaritos* and *jíbaritas* call home, and where the little *coquí* sings its lullabies.

AFTER THE STORY

Daily challenges with finances, love, faith, and redemption transcend cultural and geographical boundaries. Though this book is my story, it could be about anyone seeking the love of his parents, his God, and the pursuit of the American Dream. The last chapter ends with the passing of my biological father, but other stories go on.

After leaving Los Angeles and, later, Colorado Springs, our family moved to Virginia where I graduated from Regent University with a Master of Arts degree in Education. Shortly thereafter I became the headmaster of a half-century-old private urban academy (kindergarten through twelfth grade) in Norfolk, Virginia. At that time the school had very limited diversity. We opened our doors to also provide educational opportunities for children with learning challenges.

With the help of a dedicated faculty and administrative staff, we restructured the school's educational program to accommodate students within the school's limited finances. From the maintenance crew to the teachers, our work was a labor of love and attracted sponsorship of resources and community volunteers.

Sensitivity to community needs allowed the school to become much more representative of the city's multi-ethnic citizenry. In addition, we received support for a sports program staffed entirely by volunteers and led by Bob Mackey, an exceptional head coach. Within two years, the team won the school's first state basketball championship, resulting in student athletes receiving college scholarships. The many inspirational stories of teachers, coaches, staff, and students could fill an entire book. What an honor to know and work with them all.

My wife, Norma, and I have been in love for over fifty years. It would be a stretch of the truth if we said that every moment of our marriage was filled with bliss. Like other couples, we have had moments of stress. Still, we always find a way to talk through our issues and try to correct our mistakes. We set pride aside and accept our errors, making a commitment to change our ways.

As time has gone by and we witness the sacrifices we make for one another, we continue to grow deeper in love and have a greater appreciation for our wedding covenant. We have learned to value laughing together and the moments when we have shed tears. We have become the greatest of friends.

In retrospect, it had to be an act of God that our paths crossed and helped me win over the first-year college student who would become my wife. It wasn't a coincidence. I was divinely matched with this beautiful woman who demonstrated profound love and patience in coping with this hyper, opinionated *Boricua*.

Our three sons grew to be successful in their career endeavors and as fathers. Our greatest satisfaction has been to witness their great love for their children and extended family. My oldest, Louis, who was raised by his mother in Connecticut, petitioned the court at the age of eighteen to have his last name legally changed as his way of having a closer connection to a father and family he had never met.

Several years later, while eating at a Hartford restaurant, he was approached by one of my family members who was curious about his startling resemblance to me. When he realized he had been recognized by one of my aunts, he introduced himself and asked if she could help him contact his father. The following Christmas Eve, he welcomed us into his home and introduced me to his children. I became an instant grandparent.

Over the years, Louis has accepted our love and loved us in return. We talk and interact frequently and visit as often as we can. Because of his grace and understanding, he has become an integral part of our *familia*.

My stepfather, Daniel Sierra, returned to Puerto Rico with my mom and settled in Santa Isabel after selling their restaurant in Hartford. Originally from Cidras, Puerto Rico, he became a successful and beloved businessman in the beach community near my birthplace of El Cocal. He died of cancer at the age of sixty-nine and is buried near my grandparents and Uncle Guiso, Luis Romero, in Santa Isabel.

After my stepfather's death, Norma and I brought Mom to the States to live with us. It became our opportunity and great pleasure to care for her and regain some of the time we lost when we were apart. For nearly ten years we witnessed a side of her that had been unfamiliar to me in my youth. As a single parent, my mom had been tough, sometimes too tough, trying to make up for the lack of a father's presence in our home.

In her advanced age and fragile state, we witnessed a gentle soul, constantly thanking and kissing us whenever we provided a helping hand. We grew to cherish these special moments. They resulted in making me a more patient and loving person. These tender times brought peace and fulfillment to my heart that had long yearned for my mother's affection.

Mom also felt fulfilled and found great joy in the love she received from her grandchildren and great-grandchildren. They all referred to her as "GG," which stood for Great Grandmother. A month after her ninetieth birthday, she left us to be with her loved ones in glory.

Our dear friend, Maria Pruetzel, who had moved back to Boquerón, Puerto Rico, passed away and went to be with her Lord and her beloved son, Freddie Prinze Sr., on June 7, 2013. Maria was my spiritual *madrina* (godmother) who always had a positive word to share about life and her love for God. A kind and humble spirit, she sacrificed so much—like many Puerto Ricans of her era—to migrate to the States to create a new life. She supported her immensely talented son in his desires to succeed as a comedian, recording artist, and motion picture and television actor. Her words continue to be a great inspiration for me, and she is greatly missed.

My brother Vitín and I have visited and kept in contact over the years. He settled in Santa Isabel, where he lives in retirement near his many children and grandchildren. My older brother Guiso passed away, and Maso and I were never able to meet again after my parents' divorce. My hope is that he broke his heroin addiction and found someone to love.

My uncle and godfather, Tio Luis, also retired to Santa Isabel and took residence in my grandparents' home until his passing. During my frequent travels to Puerto Rico, I had the pleasure of speaking with him at length about his youth and later struggles in East Chicago. He shared how, as the oldest sibling, he distilled rum and sold milk to help supplement his father's income to feed his younger brother and sisters after the Great Depression. It was a matter of life and death, and they all chose to fight for their lives. Perhaps that is the reason the siblings were known as being tough and determined in character. Some would misinterpret this strength as their having a tough demeanor. But those who had the pleasure of knowing them have witnessed their gentle and hospitable hearts.

My co-worker, Moses Price, married a beautiful lady from Canada and retired from TV-30 after three decades. He continues to teach the craft of television video production to public school students and has his own production company. When we can, we visit on my travels to Connecticut.

My alma mater, Eastern Connecticut State College, became a university and honored my mentor, Dean Betty Tipton, by naming a conference center after her.

My political mentor, Maria Sanchez, was honored by Connecticut's capital city by naming a school after her and locating it near her old neighborhood in Hartford's North End. The great singing legend of Puerto Rico, Mr. Bobby Capó, and I were finally able to meet again after my embarrassing encounter with him when I was a child in the Bronx. I had the great privilege of introducing him to his adoring audience at an awards and scholarship fundraising banquet in Los Angeles. He had flown in from New York where he lived and represented Puerto Rico's Labor Department at the time.

On the night of the event and before bringing him to the microphone, I asked the audience for a moment to make a personal confession. A hush came over the attendees as they listened intently to my explanation of my childhood encounter with Mr. Capó and my subsequent admiration for his music and lyrics, which reminded me of our beloved Puerto Rico.

Bobby had not intended to sing that night but had a change of heart after my confession and sang a medley of his greatest hits, including my personal favorite "*Soñando Con Puerto Rico,*" He received a standing ovation.

After acknowledging the applause, he turned to me and said, "*Luis Rivera, eso es para que cepas quien es Bobby Capó!*" ("Luis Rivera, that's so you'll know who Bobby Capó is!")

Everyone laughed and cheered, including me, as I gave him two thumbs up.

Civic and Hispanic community involvement has been important to me since my teen years and continued throughout the years I lived in LA. One of the many community groups I worked with was the *Noche de San Juan* committee, which held the before-mentioned annual awards and scholarship banquet. This banquet was the culmination of activities celebrated at the daytime beach gathering known as *El Dia De San Juan*.

San Juan Day was celebrated at LA's Cabrillo Beach with over fifty thousand Latinos reuniting with friends and sharing their *lechon asado* (roasted pig), *salsa* music, and well wishes. The evening event's organizers consisted mainly of Puerto Rican businesspersons and was attended by professional baseball players, actors, and prominent citizens. They produced an annual awards and scholarship banquet recognizing community leaders and artists who provided positive visibility to the Puerto Rican community, as well as providing scholarships to college-bound students.

Both events were held on the same weekend near the end of June. Some of the well-known Puerto Rican artists who were honored included multi-award-winning actress Rita Moreno, guitar virtuoso Jose Feliciano, internationally renowned vocalist, TV director, and public servant Bobby Capó, and many others. They graced the nearly five-hundred attendees with their presence and were presented with awards.

On December 14, 2004, with the leadership and benevolence of comedian and actor George Lopez, the Hollywood Walk of Fame honored the comedic career of the late Freddie Prinze Sr. with his own star. Norma and I attended the event on behalf of Freddie's mother and were reunited with friends we hadn't seen in nearly twenty-five years since leaving LA.

During our visit, we attended the production of the *George Lopez Show*. The actor/comedian was gracious and introduced Norma, my friend Alex Soto, and me to his audience and co-workers. He invited us to his studio office after the show. We were touched by George's story of how Freddie had been an influence in his comedic career. I was personally fascinated by the air-brushed electric guitar hanging on his wall, given to him by Rock and Roll Hall of Famer and Latin fusion superstar Carlos Santana.

After nearly thirty years apart, entertainer and recording artist Tony Orlando and I were able to visit once again when he was interviewed at the CBN television studio in Virginia Beach, Virginia. We enjoyed the morning together and reminisced about our days in Hollywood and Freddie Prinze's tragic death. Tony had written a memoir in which he mentioned meeting me at the hospital where Freddy Prinze Sr. had died. He referred to our uncanny resemblance to one another and that we could have passed for brothers. In fact, many of the news articles and books written about Freddie's death included my picture captioned with Tony Orlando's name.

It has been a great pleasure and a challenge living between Puerto Rico and the States. My experiences have left me with a better understanding and admiration for my fellow citizens, their cultures, and beautiful landscapes. There is so much more that can be accomplished when we are united and there is mutual respect and love for one another.

This is but a short phase of my life, as I continue to take steps in my journey. There are still many challenges ahead for me and my family to face. As we sojourn through this adventure we call life, I have learned we must love one another and conquer fear by trusting and believing in a Greater Power. After trying to accomplish the American Dream on my terms, I came to a realization I needed help from caring individuals and, most importantly, our merciful God. He has walked hand in hand with me through my trials and tribulations, and He looks forward to doing the same for you.

ABOUT THE AUTHOR

Luis Alberto Rivera Colón, a native of Puerto Rico, relocated to the States from humble beginnings. In his youth he contended with the rewards and hardships of a bilingual/bicultural upbringing (Spanish/English). Rivera's hunger to help the less fortunate led him to be nurtured and mentored by many local activists, resulting in an early awareness of community politics and the human rights struggles of the late 60s and early 70s.

While afflicted with a learning disorder, he received help from concerned teachers and community leaders enabling him to enroll in college. Between studies, Rivera counseled Hispanic high school students and joined efforts to increase recruitment of minority college students. During two riots in the late 60s, Luis served on a mayoral task force to bring calm to the city of Hartford, Connecticut. He served his college practicum as an aide to a state senator from an inner-city district.

After Rivera graduated from college, an NBC-affiliated television station recognized his potential, even though he had no formal training in journalism or broadcasting. He became one of a few minority television personalities in the New England states. Less than three years later, Rivera was recruited to join a network-owned and operated television news team in Hollywood, California.

What followed was a life of challenges in the fast lane, meeting and working with celebrities. Rivera's sensitivity to the community was recognized by many civic and ethnic groups, including Native Americans. After witnessing the tragic death of a young television and motion picture artist, Luis had a life-changing experience and left the Hollywood scene.

Rivera, now retired, resides in Virginia with his wife of nearly 50 years. They have three sons and numerous grandchildren and great-grandchildren. He continues his involvement in the Hispanic community, civic leadership, and Christian service organizations.

ACKNOWLEDGEMENTS

I offer profound thanks to my friends: Cristóbal Krusen, founder of Messenger Films (messengerfilms.com) for helping me express my thoughts in writing;

Evelyn Wagoner for her excellent editing and mentorship in the KPC Writers Group;

Joe and Lynne Kohm of the C.S. Lewis Institute Fellows Program for helping me better understand and commit to discipleship;

the Water of Life Prayer Line who helped me understand the importance and practice of prayer.

Finally, thanks to all my extended family and friends (*si—estoy hablando de ti*) who helped shape my life and provided their prayers and *bendiciónes* along the way.

LIVING BETWEEN CULTURES

GLOSSARY

Abuela	Grandmother
Abuelo	Grandfather
Abuelos	Grandparents
Adobo	Spices used in cooking that can include garlic, salt, black pepper, and oregano
Aguacates	Avocados
Agua de Florida	Florida water; a rubbing alcohol mixed with water that smelled of citrus flowers and cinnamon
Almacén	Warehouse
Americano	An American
Amigas	Female friends
Aquí Me Quedo	"I'll Stay Here"
Arroz con gandules	Yellow rice and pigeon peas
Arroz con pollo	Yellow rice and chicken
Asopado	A heavy rice soup that can include meat or seafood and can be referred to as "Asopao"
Asopado de pollo	A heavy rice soup with chicken
Ataques de nervios	Nervous convulsions

"¡Ay bendito!"	Phrase or exclamation used in a variety of circumstances that can indicate sympathy or frustration
Bacalaítos	Codfish fritters
Bendición	A request for a blessing, a sign of respect young Puerto Ricans show their elders, especially their parents and family members
Billete	In the context of this book, indicates a Puerto Rico National Lottery ticket
Bochinche	Gossip
Bolero	A slow romantic dance
Boricua(s)	Boriquen was the native Taino name for Puerto Rico; sons and daughters of Puerto Rico are known as Boricuas
Borinquen	Derived from the native Taino name for Puerto Rico, Boriquen
Buenas noches	Goodnight
Caballeros	Gentlemen
Café con leche	Coffee with milk
¡Cállense!	"Be quiet!"

Campesinos	Country people or farm workers
Cangrejos	Crabs
¡Caramba!	An exclamation used when one is frustrated or something goes wrong
Caravana de acabe	A caravan signifying the end of a harvest
Carro publico	A public car; car for hire
Cacerolas	Cooking pots
Chiapas	A southern state of Mexico
Chihuahua	The largest state of Mexico.
Cocal	A coconut grove
Colonia	A colony typically named after its owners, as in *Colonia Alomar*
Cocos	Coconuts
Compadre	Name used to indicate a man's relationship with the father and mother of a child that has been baptized by him
Coquí	Tiny tree frog revered in Puerto Rico and known for its distinct sound
Cortijo y Su Combo	A musical combo led by Rafael Cortijo

Cuatro	Four; in the context of this book, refers to a small traditional guitar
Dios el Todopoderoso	God the All Powerful and Mighty Protector
Dios te bendiga	"God bless you." In the context of this book, refers to the answer given when someone asks for a blessing (*La Bendición*)
Discusiones	Arguments
El barbero	Barber
El Día De San Juan	San Juan Day (Saint John the Baptist Day) celebrated by Puerto Ricans on or near June 24 of each year
El hombre de la casa	The man of the house.
Fajitas de pollo	Chicken fajitas
Familia	Family
Fichas	Domino game pieces/stones
Fiesta de bautismo	Baptism party
Flamboyán	The Royal Poinciana tree
Flan	An egg custard dessert
Gringo	A term used to refer to a foreigner, more specifically Americans; not intended as a derogatory term in common usage

Guadalajara	Capital of Mexico's state of Jalisco
Hacienda	Plantation or estate
Huevos con chorizo	Scrambled eggs and spicy Mexican pork sausage
Jalisco	A state in western Mexico
Jíbaro or Jíbarito	Farm worker; a country person that works with the earth and symbolizes a humble, hardworking, and traditional lifestyle
Ladrón	Thief
La Escondida	The Hidden Female
La Fonda	A small restaurant that can be found in a boarding house
La Frontera	The Frontier
Lamento Borincano	The Puerto Rican Lament—a popular song written by Rafael Hernández Marín that speaks of a country person (a Jibarito) struggling to survive
La policía	The police
Lechón Asado	Roasted pig
Lagartijos	Small green lizards
Letrina	Latrine or outhouse toilet
Loco	Crazy
Lotería	Lottery

Machete	A long bladed cutting knife used as a tool in cutting sugar cane
Machismo	Manliness
Madrinas	Godmothers
Mama	Mother
Mayordomo	Manager of the sugar cane cutting operation
Me Lo Dijo Adela	Adela Told Me
Menudo	Beef tripe stew that can resemble the Boricua mondongo stew
Mi amor	My love
Mi angel	My angel
Mi cielo	My heaven
Mi hijo(s)	My son; a shortened version *"Mijo(s)"*
Mi maestro	My teacher
Mofongo	A dish made with mashed fried green plantains and can include meat or seafood
Mortadella	Italian hard salami
Mosquitero	Mosquito netting placed over a bed and typically tied to bed posts
Muchacho	Boy
Noche de Paz	Silent Night (Christmas carol)

Noche de San Juan	Night of San Juan
Nueva York	New York
Nuyorican(s)	Person(s) born (or raised) in New York City to Puerto Rican parents
Oro Negro	Black Gold
Padrino	Godfather
Pan de agua or *manteca*	Bread baked in small neighborhood bakeries (panaderías) and visibly resembling Italian or French bread, but with their own unique taste.
Papas sin sal	Potatoes without salt
Papi	Father
Pasteles de carne	Meat pies
Pegado (Pegao)	Attached; in the context of this book, refers to someone very close to another person.
Pentecostales	Pentecostals
Picador de caña	Worker that cuts sugarcane
Piragua	Snow cone
Piragüero	Person dispensing snow cones
Pitorro	Homemade rum
Poquito lento	A little slow

Pollo asada	Broiled or roasted chicken
Pueblo	Town
Ruiseñor	Nightingale bird
Salsa	Sauce; also refers to the New York City rhythmic music rendition of the Greater Antilles islands (Puerto Rico, Cuba and Dominican Republic)
San Cristóbal	St. Christopher
Santa Isabel	Saint Isabel (a town in south-central coast of Puerto Rico)
Seguro Social	The United States Social Security program
Señora	Woman (married)
Señorita	Young woman; can also signify a female's virginity
Sentimiento	Feelings
Sinvergüenzas	Shameless
Sofrito	The seasoning base of many Puerto Rican dishes that can consist of chopped tomatoes, green and sweet peppers, onions, cilantro, and garlic
Sopa	Soup

Spanglish	Slang term for a mixture of Spanish and English
Tamarindo	Tamarind, commonly used in juices and syrup
Tecato	A heroin addict
Telefono	Telephone
Tío	Uncle
Tía	Aunt
Tostones	Sliced fried green plantains
¡Un paradiso	Italian for "a paradise"
Vicio	Bad habit or vice

(Phrases)

"*¡Dios mío!*"
"My God!"

"*Ese es un buen muchacho.*"
"That's a good boy."

"*¿Está bien?*"
"It's all right?"

"*Estoy aquí para ayudarles.*"
"I'm here to help you."

"*Estoy orgullosa de ti.*"
"I'm proud of you."

"*Gracias, Papa.*"
"Thank you, Father."

"Hay muchos caciques y pocos indios por aquí."
"There are many chiefs and not enough Indians
around here."

"Juanito Bobo!"
"A silly boy."

"¿Muchacho, que haces tú aquí?"
"What're you doing here, boy?"

"Nenes traviesos. ¡Como los amo!"
"Mischievous boys. How I love them!"

"¡No se apuren!"
"Don't worry!"

"¡No estoy aquí para hacerles daño!"
"I'm not here to harm you!"

*"¡Óyeme, Tomás! ¡Te ves bien, amigo,
con la señora!"*
"Hey, Tomás! You're looking good
with the missus, friend!"

*"Padre, perdóname si en algún
momento te ofendí."*
"Father, forgive me if at any moment
I offended you."

"¡Qué buen muchacho!"
"What a good boy!"

"¿Quién?"
"Who?"

"*¿Quién sabe?*"
"Who knows?"

¡Sin dudas!"
"No doubt about it'!"

"*Sí, tío.*"
"Yes, uncle."

"*Tate quieto, muchacho, o te pongo la dita.*"
"Be still, boy, or I'll put the gourd bowl on you."

"*Tu papá te va a dar una pela cuando llegues
a tu casa ...*"
"Your dad's gonna' give you a spanking when you
get home ...'"

"*Ven acá, muchacho.*"
"Come over here, boy."

"*Ya era tiempo, ¿Cierto?*"
"It's about time, really!"

Made in the USA
Middletown, DE
08 October 2020